Sacred Suffering

A STUDY ON THE BOOK OF JOB

This study belongs to:

_____

_____

KATIE DAVIDSON

Even if we do not get the answers we want, God will give us the answers we need.

Study Suggestions

We believe that the Bible is true, trustworthy, and timeless and that it is vitally important for all believers. These study suggestions are intended to help you more effectively study Scripture as you seek to know and love God through His Word.

SUGGESTED STUDY TOOLS

- ☐ Bible

- ☐ Double-spaced, printed copy of the Scripture passages that this study covers (You can use a website like www.biblegateway.com to copy the text of a passage and print out a double-spaced copy to be able to mark on easily.)

- ☐ Journal to write notes or prayers

- ☐ Pens, colored pencils, and highlighters

- ☐ Dictionary to look up unfamiliar words

HOW TO USE THIS STUDY

 ### Pray

Begin your study time in prayer. Ask God to reveal Himself to you, help you understand what you are reading, and transform you with His Word (Psalm 119:18).

 ### Read Scripture

Before you read what is written in each day of the study itself, read the assigned passages of Scripture for that day. Use your double-spaced copy to circle, underline, highlight, draw arrows, and mark in any way you would like to help you dig deeper as you work through a passage.

 ### Memorize Scripture

Each week of the study begins with a memory verse. You may want to write the verse down and put it in a place where you will see it often. We also recommend spending a few minutes memorizing the verse before you complete each day's study material.

 ### Read Study Content

Read the daily written content provided for the current study day.

 ### Respond

Answer the questions that appear at the end of each study day.

How to Study the Bible

The inductive method provides tools for deeper and more intentional Bible study. To study the Bible inductively, work through the steps below after reading background information on the book.

01 Observation & Comprehension

KEY QUESTION: WHAT DOES THE TEXT SAY?

After reading the daily Scripture in its entirety at least once, begin working with smaller portions of the Scripture. Read a passage of Scripture repetitively, and then mark the following items in the text:

- Key or repeated words and ideas
- Key themes
- Transition words (e.g., therefore, but, because, if/then, likewise, etc.)
- Lists
- Comparisons and contrasts
- Commands
- Unfamiliar words (look these up in a dictionary)
- Questions you have about the text

02 Interpretation

KEY QUESTION: WHAT DOES THE TEXT MEAN?

Once you have annotated the text, work through the following steps to help you interpret its meaning:

- Read the passage in other versions for a better understanding of the text.
- Read cross-references to help interpret Scripture with Scripture.
- Paraphrase or summarize the passage to check for understanding.
- Identify how the text reflects the metanarrative of Scripture, which is the story of creation, fall, redemption, and restoration.
- Read trustworthy commentaries if you need further insight into the meaning of the passage.

Application

Bible study is not merely an intellectual pursuit. The truths about God, ourselves, and the gospel that we discover in Scripture should produce transformation in our hearts and lives. Answer the following questions and prompts as you consider what you have learned in your study:

- What attributes of God's character are revealed in the passage?

- Consider places where the text directly states the character of God, as well as how His character is revealed through His words and actions.

- What do I learn about myself in light of who God is?

- Consider how you fall short of God's character, how the text reveals your sin nature, and what it says about your new identity in Christ.

- How should this truth change me?

- A passage of Scripture may contain direct commands telling us what to do or warnings about sins to avoid in order to help us grow in holiness. Other times, our application flows out of seeing ourselves in light of God's character. As we pray and reflect on how God is calling us to change in light of His Word, we should be asking questions like, "How should I pray for God to change my heart?" and "What practical steps can I take toward cultivating habits of holiness?"

The Attributes of God

Eternal

God has no beginning and no end. He always was, always is, and always will be.

HAB. 1:12 / REV. 1:8 / ISA. 41:4

Faithful

God is incapable of anything but fidelity. He is loyally devoted to His plan and purpose.

2 TIM. 2:13 / DEUT. 7:9 / HEB. 10:23

Good

God is pure; there is no defilement in Him. He is unable to sin, and all He does is good.

GEN. 1:31 / PS. 34:8 / PS. 107:1

Gracious

God is kind, giving us gifts and benefits we do not deserve.

2 KINGS 13:23 / PS. 145:8 ISA. 30:18

Holy

God is undefiled and unable to be in the presence of defilement. He is sacred and set-apart.

REV. 4:8 / LEV. 19:2 / HAB. 1:13

Incomprehensible and Transcendent

God is high above and beyond human understanding. He is unable to be fully known.

PS. 145:3 / ISA. 55:8–9 ROM. 11:33–36

Immutable

God does not change. He is the same yesterday, today, and tomorrow.

1 SAM. 15:29 / ROM. 11:29 JAMES 1:17

Infinite

God is limitless. He exhibits all of His attributes perfectly and boundlessly.

ROM. 11:33–36 / ISA. 40:28 PS. 147:5

Jealous

God is desirous of receiving the praise and affection He rightly deserves.

EXOD. 20:5 / DEUT. 4:23–24 JOSH. 24:19

Just

God governs in perfect justice. He acts in accordance with justice. In Him, there is no wrongdoing or dishonesty.

ISA. 61:8 / DEUT. 32:4 / PS. 146:7–9

Loving

God is eternally, enduringly, steadfastly loving and affectionate. He does not forsake or betray His covenant love.

JOHN 3:16 / EPH. 2:4–5 / 1 JOHN 4:16

Merciful

God is compassionate, withholding from us the wrath that we deserve.

TITUS 3:5 / PS. 25:10 LAM. 3:22–23

Omnipotent

God is all-powerful;
His strength is unlimited.

MATT. 19:26 / JOB 42:1-2
JER. 32:27

Omnipresent

God is everywhere;
His presence is near
and permeating.

PROV. 15:3 / PS. 139:7-10
JER. 23:23-24

Omniscient

God is all-knowing;
there is nothing
unknown to Him.

PS. 147:4 / I JOHN 3:20
HEB. 4:13

Patient

God is long-suffering and
enduring. He gives ample
opportunity for people
to turn toward Him.

ROM. 2:4 / 2 PET. 3:9 / PS. 86:15

Self-Existent

God was not created
but exists by His
power alone.

PS. 90:1-2 / JOHN 1:4 / JOHN 5:26

Self-Sufficient

God has no needs
and depends on
nothing, but everything
depends on God.

ISA. 40:28-31 / ACTS 17:24-25
PHIL. 4:19

Sovereign

God governs over
all things; He is in
complete control.

COL. 1:17 / PS. 24:1-2
1 CHRON. 29:11-12

Truthful

God is our measurement
of what is fact. By Him
we are able to discern
true and false.

JOHN 3:33 / ROM. 1:25 / JOHN 14:6

Wise

God is infinitely
knowledgeable and
is judicious with
His knowledge.

ISA. 46:9-10 / ISA. 55:9 / PROV. 3:19

Wrathful

God stands in opposition
to all that is evil. He enacts
judgment according to
His holiness, righteousness,
and justice.

PS. 69:24 / JOHN 3:36 / ROM. 1:18

Timeline of Scripture

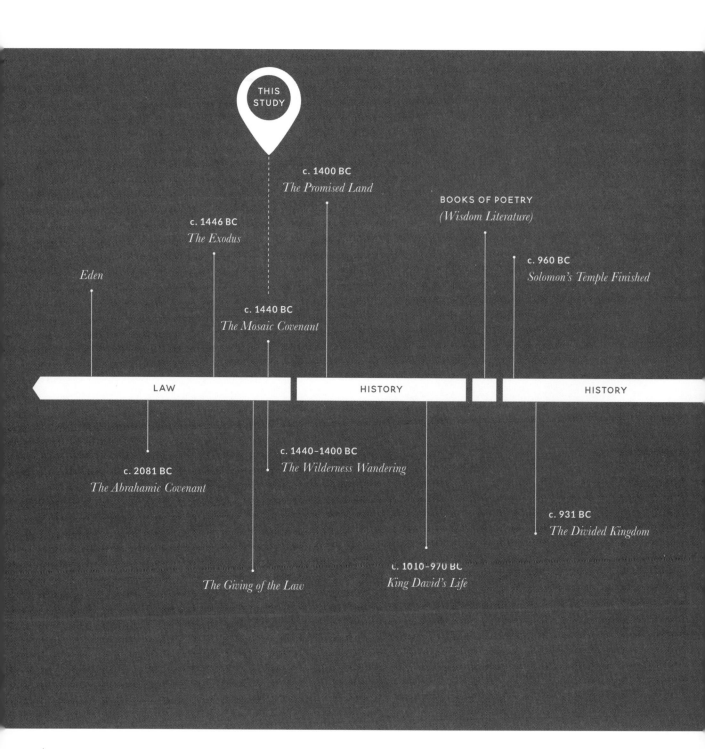

THIS STUDY

c. 1400 BC
The Promised Land

BOOKS OF POETRY
(Wisdom Literature)

c. 1446 BC
The Exodus

c. 960 BC
Solomon's Temple Finished

Eden

c. 1440 BC
The Mosaic Covenant

LAW

HISTORY

HISTORY

c. 2081 BC
The Abrahamic Covenant

c. 1440–1400 BC
The Wilderness Wandering

c. 931 BC
The Divided Kingdom

The Giving of the Law

c. 1010–970 BC
King David's Life

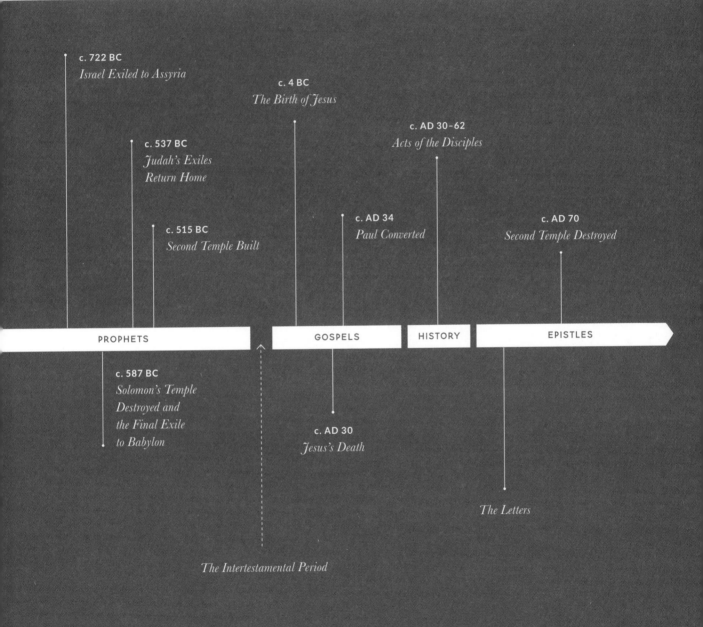

c. 722 BC
Israel Exiled to Assyria

c. 4 BC
The Birth of Jesus

c. AD 30–62
Acts of the Disciples

c. 537 BC
*Judah's Exiles
Return Home*

c. AD 34
Paul Converted

c. AD 70
Second Temple Destroyed

c. 515 BC
Second Temple Built

PROPHETS

GOSPELS

HISTORY

EPISTLES

c. 587 BC
*Solomon's Temple
Destroyed and
the Final Exile
to Babylon*

c. AD 30
Jesus's Death

The Letters

The Intertestamental Period

Metanarrative of Scripture

Creation

In the beginning, God created the universe. He made the world and everything in it. He created humans in His own image to be His representatives on the earth.

Fall

The first humans, Adam and Eve, disobeyed God by eating from the fruit of the Tree of Knowledge of Good and Evil. Their disobedience impacted the whole world. The punishment for sin is death, and because of Adam's original sin, all humans are sinful and condemned to death.

Redemption

God sent His Son to become a human and redeem His people. Jesus Christ lived a sinless life but died on the cross to pay the penalty for sin. He resurrected from the dead and ascended into heaven. All who put their faith in Jesus are saved from death and freely receive the gift of eternal life.

Restoration

One day, Jesus Christ will return again and restore all that sin destroyed. He will usher in a new heaven and new earth where all who trust in Him will live eternally with glorified bodies in the presence of God.

*Even as tides change and waves
of pain roar around us,
God is enough in any season.*

Outline of Job

Job's Tragedies

INTRODUCTION TO JOB
Job 1:1–5

JOB'S TESTS
Job 1:6–2:10

JOB'S COMFORTERS
Job 2:11–13

Job's Wrestling

FIRST ROUND OF SPEECHES
Job 3–14

SECOND ROUND OF SPEECHES
Job 15–21

THIRD ROUND OF SPEECHES
Job 22–31

ELIHU'S OBSERVANCE
Job 32–37

Job's Redemption

GOD SPEAKS TO JOB
Job 38–41

JOB'S REPENTANCE + REDEMPTION
Job 42

Scripture Memory

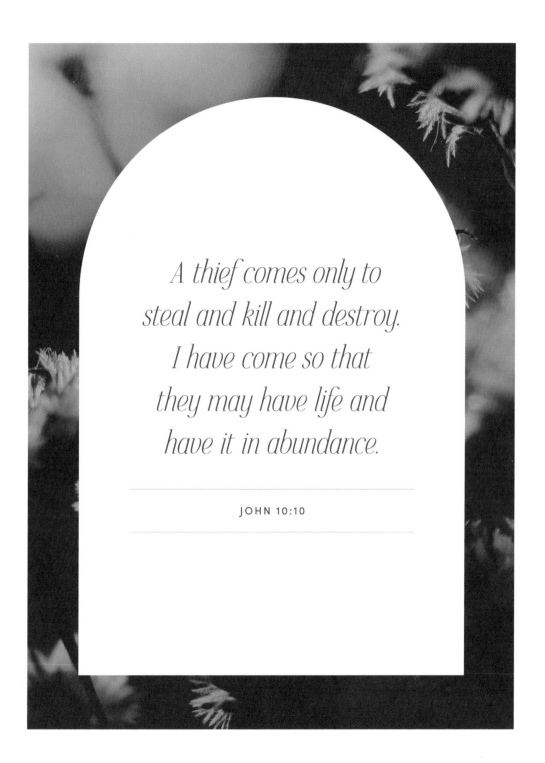

*A thief comes only to
steal and kill and destroy.
I have come so that
they may have life and
have it in abundance.*

JOHN 10:10

Now My Eyes Have Seen You

When your worst fears are realized and your nightmares see the light of day, where is God? It is no secret that seasons of suffering can leave us feeling alone and even confused. We want answers. We want a way out. We long for comfort and relief.

Thankfully, in God's great care for us, He gave us the book of Job to help us navigate our questions and better understand our longings. However, Job does not offer the clear-cut answers we may hope for. In fact, God may seem even more mysterious after studying this book. But even if we do not get the answers we want, God will give us the answers we need. He expands our perspective of His power and glory. Our comfort is found in trusting His control and resting in His provision. The answers we seek lie not in the book of Job but in the grand redemptive story of the gospel. The answers lie in Jesus Christ.

Maybe you are reading this study because you are in a season of suffering. Maybe you have dear friends walking through a hard season, and you would like to support them. Maybe you want to dive deeper into a book of the Bible you have not yet studied. The harsh truth of our lives on earth is that all of us are likely in one of three seasons: coming out of a season of suffering, sitting in a season of suffering, or heading toward one. The book of Job teaches us that even as tides change and waves of pain roar around us, God is enough in any season.

How to Read the Book of Job

The book of Job is unique in many ways, including its authorship, timeline, and genre. We are not sure who wrote Job, but some scholars believe it was penned by Moses around 1440 BC, before most of Genesis was written. In chronological studies of the Bible, Job is read toward the beginning of the reading plan. This is because scholars

Even if we do not get the answers we want, God will give us the answers we need.

WEEK ONE | DAY ONE

believe the events of Job took place before 2100 BC—after the Flood and before God's covenant with Abraham. This book joins Proverbs, Ecclesiastes, Psalms, and the Song of Songs in the genre of wisdom literature. This genre of Scripture seeks to gather and obtain wisdom for everyday facets of life. In Job, we gain wisdom to specifically apply to suffering and justice.

Like other books in wisdom literature, Job utilizes poetry throughout the text. Unlike modern poetry that we are familiar with, Hebrew poetry does not rely on syllable count or rhyme. Instead, readers will notice wordplay, vivid imagery, and ideas develop throughout multiple lines of poetry.

As we study Job, we must also remember that poetry is not always meant to be taken literally. Often, authors will use poetic devices like similes, metaphors, and imagery to describe a concept that would fall flat if written in prose. As you read, allow your mind to imagine the picture that the author paints. What is the author communicating through this imagery? What does this image reveal about God or the human condition? Poetry prompts us to slow down and savor the words, knowing that they were chosen carefully and artistically to communicate a specific truth. Through poetry, we are able to better feel the tension within Job's heart as he attempts to understand his heartache.

Who and What is the Book of Job About?

So who is Job? He is a man of integrity (Job 1:1). He loves the Lord and does all that he can to obey Him. However, when his family dies and his comfort is stripped away, Job finds difficulty reconciling what he knows about God with his current agony. As we read Job, we see that this book is much less about suffering than we may anticipate. Instead, the book primarily explores God's justice. The characters in Job wrestle with questions like: Does all suffering come from disobedience to God? How does God treat those He loves? Who causes suffering? Where is God in my suffering?

In the book of Job, we witness Job wrestle with his faith. We see him doubt God's goodness. We see him question God's control.

We see him in anguish, in silence, in anger, in frustration, in fear, and in despair. His feelings of suffering cover the breadth of our own suffering. In Job's cries, we hear our own. If justice were the ocean, we wade in the shallow waters by the shore. God holds all knowledge, all power, and all dominion over His creation. We cannot fathom swimming in the deepest depths of the sea—nor were we created to do so.

Seasons of despair cause us to lie exposed. Finally, our pride is pummeled, and we realize our need. Under wave after wave of heartache, we become desperate for air. It is here that we often cry to God—right in the midst of our deepest pain. In God's grace, He rescues us, and along the way, we learn that He is worthy of our trust and obedience. We learn that there are answers in His Word. We learn to heed His tender voice and rest our weight on His promises. No longer do we tread water in our own strength; He holds us up.

In Job 42:5, Job says to God, "I had heard reports about you, but now my eyes have seen you." The book of Job teaches us that we move closer to God even in the midst of pain. Job begs us to ask ourselves: *What can we learn about God in this present suffering?* We learn to rely less on our own strength and understanding and more on the very God who gives the sea its boundaries. Ultimately, the cries of Job are answered in Jesus Christ—the One who is lowly and humble in heart, the Friend of the outcast, the Healer of the hurting, and the Calmer of our storms.

> ❝
>
> ULTIMATELY, THE CRIES OF JOB ARE ANSWERED IN JESUS CHRIST.

1. Have you read the book of Job before? If so, what do you remember learning? If you have not, what questions do you have?

2. What does justice mean to you? Do you believe God is just?

3. Reflect on your last season of suffering. What did you learn about God?

NOTES

ATTRIBUTE OF GOD I'M MEDITATING ON TODAY

REMEMBER THIS

25

Black Sea

Caspian Sea

Mediterranean Sea

Uz[†]

CHALDEA

•Teman

Persian Gulf

•Medina

Red Sea

ARABIA

Sheba

Arabian Sea

Map of Uz

Where does the book of Job take place? Job is especially unique in that the book does not take place in Israel. In chapter 1, we learn that Job lives in the land of Uz, which is east of Israel. Therefore, this book holds no significance in the timeline of God's chosen nation. However, that does not negate the importance of Job. By existing outside of Israel's narrative, Job's story allows readers to focus more deeply on the themes present within this book, like God's justice, glory, and presence in the midst of suffering.

Editor's Note: Along with the first four books of the Pentateuch (Genesis, Exodus, Leviticus, and Numbers), Job is believed to be one of the earliest-written books in Scripture. However, unlike the books of the Pentateuch, the book of Job is not primarily concerned with historical events; instead, it can be understood as wisdom literature, which seeks to answer big questions about God, human beings, and the order of the world. For these two reasons, scholars remain largely uncertain about the location of the specific places referenced within the book of Job. However, this map gives us a rough idea of where these locations may have been during Job's lifetime.

UZ[†] — *Where Job lived and where his sufferings took place (Job 1:1)*

TEMAN — *The city in Edom where Eliphaz was from (Job 2:11)*

ARABIA — *Where Zophar and Bildad were likely from (Job 2:11)*

SABA* — *Where the Sabeans came from (Job 1:15)*

CHALDEA — *Where the Chaldeans came from (Job 1:17)*

LOCATION UNKNOWN — *Where Elihu was from (Job 32:2)*

---

*Job 1:15 describes "the Sabeans," and Job 6:19 describes "the traveling merchants of Sheba." In the original Hebrew, the same word is used to describe both of these people groups. However, scholars remain divided on where this people group would have been located. Some believe they came from far southern Arabia (marked as "Sheba" on this map), while others believe they came from further north in Arabia, perhaps near the city of Medina on this map. Due to scholarly uncertainty, we have included both possible locations.

† Uncertain location

Meet Job

Why do Bad Things Happen to Good People?

This is a question we may find ourselves asking as we meet Job, the main character of this book. It is important to remember that Job is not just a person from history's past. As silly as it sounds, we must remember that Job was a real man. Job was a husband, a parent, and a man of success and honor. He was revered, and he held clout among his peers. In many ways, Job was a picture of prosperity in his community. As we venture through Job, remembering Job's humanness is key. We will see this protagonist suffer. We will see him wrestle with his faith. And ultimately, we will see him humbled and restored by God.

Unlike many heroes of the Old Testament, we are not given Job's genealogy. We are not sure what the name "Job" symbolizes. In the same way, we have little context for Job's homeland. His story takes place east of Israel in the land of Uz. Because Job's story takes place outside of Israel, in many ways, the book of Job may seem to be an outlier in the Old Testament. However, by existing apart from Israel, we remember that God is not only the God of the Hebrews. He is the God of the world. His gracious hand remained on every nation and every person in biblical times, just as it does for us today.

In our text today, we also learn that Job was a blessed man. He had seven sons and three daughters, a large family he was faithful to care for. In biblical times, these sons and daughters were indicative of family legacy; Job's name and character would be remembered for generations. Job also gained much wealth during his lifetime. We see vast numbers of sheep, camels, oxen, and donkeys mentioned in the text. In those days, wealth was not measured in dollars and cents but in livestock. Those reading this text in the ancient world would likely have been impressed by Job's success.

But this success did not drive Job; instead, our introduction to Job focuses mostly on his character. Scripture tells us that Job was a man of complete integrity (Job 1:1).

Without Jesus, our world would have no hope.

WEEK ONE | DAY TWO

He sought after God with not only his heart but with his actions as well. In Job 1:4–5, we see evidence of Job's reverence for the Lord and care for his family. Job sacrificed to God on behalf of his children's theoretical sins. Just in case they had committed evil, Job acted as a mediator. He pleaded with God for the sake of those he loved. He was not reactive to sin, but instead, he was proactive. And even more, we learn that this is Job's regular habit. His life was marked by devotion to the Lord.

As we continue to learn more about Job's story, we must remember these details. Though he was the greatest in the land, Job was not consumed with power. Job's eyes were turned toward God. This will be a consistent theme throughout the book of Job. We must also remember that though Job loved God, he was not sinless. Job was still human, still flesh, and still sinful. Jesus is the only man who was sinless—the only man who persevered through trial after trial and did not turn His face from God's. Let us look at Job with a balanced approach. Yes, he was a man who honored God and served Him with all his strength, but Job was not perfect. Only Jesus is.

If Job was such a righteous man, then you may be wondering why so much harm came upon him. The question, "Why do bad things happen to good people?" is a valid and real question that addresses sin's sting in our hearts. We see brokenness all around us. We see a shattered world. We see school shootings, terrorist attacks, fatal illnesses, children lost, relational dysfunction, and suicide. We see trusted structures tumble under lie after lie. Without Jesus, our world would have no hope. However, God allowed bad things to happen to the best person—His Son—so that we may have a light to cling to in the darkness.

Jesus secured profound victory over sin and death while also experiencing its effects here on earth. He was tempted like we are. He was hurt, mocked, beaten, betrayed, and crucified—yet He never sinned (Hebrews 4:15). Jesus rose from the dead three days later, unlocking grace upon grace for those who trust in Him. Jesus is more than our Savior; He is our good friend—a comforter who has walked in our shoes. In the coming chapters of Job, we will see tragedy befall our main character. We will see his wealth demolished and his family killed. We will see him beg for relief in agony. We will see him question God. But be assured—a light is coming.

> JESUS IS MORE THAN OUR SAVIOR; HE IS OUR GOOD FRIEND— A COMFORTER WHO HAS WALKED IN OUR SHOES.

1. How would you describe Job (the person) to someone who has never read this book?

2. Read Hebrews 4:14–16. What do you learn about Jesus from these verses? How does Jesus sympathize with us in our suffering and temptation?

3. If someone asked you, "Why do bad things happen to good people?" how would you respond?

ATTRIBUTE OF GOD I'M MEDITATING ON TODAY

REMEMBER THIS

Satan's First Test

PRACTICE THIS WEEK'S MEMORY VERSE + READ JOB: 1:6–12

Today, we are transported into the heavenly realm. We become a fly on the wall in the throneroom of God, observing a conversation between Him and several of His angels. There, we find a surprising guest — Satan.

Satan is the same enemy referenced throughout the Bible from beginning to end. He is the enemy who deceives Adam and Eve in the garden of Eden (Genesis 3) and who will ultimately be defeated by Jesus when He returns to rid the world of evil (Revelation 20:10) and fully establish His kingdom (Revelation 22:3–5). When God questions Satan's whereabouts, he reports that he spends his time "roaming through the earth…and walking around on it" (Job 1:7). His mission? To steal, kill, and destroy anything of eternal value (John 10:10). He wants to turn hearts away from God and distract us from disciple-making. Like a lion prowling in the savanna for prey, we see that Satan actively searches for souls to torment.

And what is most surprising about this passage is that God actually proposes a new target to Satan — Job (Job 1:8). God does not suggest Job because he has gravely sinned or blasphemed His name. No, God affirms Job's character. God bestows upon Job a title reserved only for prophets and patriarchs of the faith like Abraham and Moses — "my servant" (Psalm 105:42, Numbers 12:7). Can you imagine being complimented by God? Let that soak in a little. We learn that the God of all splendor and majesty utters Job's name on His lips — and not only that, He calls Job "a man of perfect integrity" (Job 1:8). God knows the loyalty cemented in Job's heart.

Satan jumps at the opportunity. The potential to turn one of God's most faithful servants away from Him sounds too good to pass up. Satan belittles Job's loyalty with the question, "Does Job fear God for nothing?" (Job 1:9). This is a question we also must ask ourselves. In other words, *If our wealth disappears, if our comforts vanish, if we lie in pain for the rest of our days, will we still worship the God we call the Lord of our lives?* Satan proposes that Job loves God solely because of His blessings. Without God's hedge of protection around him, Satan believes Job will surely curse God (Job 1:11). This attack

Even if we have nothing, even in despair, God is still worthy of our praise.

WEEK ONE | DAY THREE

is not only meant for Job but is also an attack on God. By doubting Job's love for God, Satan doubts God's glory.

God allows Satan to afflict Job with suffering but only within the bounds He permits. At this point in the story, God sets the following boundaries: Satan can take anything from Job, but he is not allowed to harm Job physically. Here, we learn an important, applicable truth. God sets the boundaries for Satan. As such, Satan cannot do anything outside of the Lord's knowledge or permission (Isaiah 14:27). God holds all authority. Though God does allow us to see trials and experience hardship, God is not the One inflicting this evil—that is Satan. However, the question remains: why does God permit Job to suffer in the first place?

We are never given a clear answer. We do know many things to be true about God. He is all-knowing (omniscient), all-powerful (omnipotent), and everywhere at once (omnipresent). This means that before God even mentioned Job's name to Satan, God knew the outcome of Job's test. God's breadth and depth of knowledge are much more than our minds can comprehend. And just as He is bigger and greater, so are His decisions. Through the prophet Isaiah, God reminds us, "For as heaven is higher than earth, so my ways are higher than your ways, and my thoughts than your thoughts" (Isaiah 55:9). Though we may not know God's purpose behind testing Job, we can trust God's eternal perspective. We can know that these present trials will be for Job's greater good and for God's glory.

Upon more reflection, perhaps we can see that the point of Job's suffering is to proclaim to us, and to all people, that even if we have nothing, even in despair, God is still worthy of our praise. God foreknows the future—when His Son, Jesus, will defeat Satan once and for all. In the book of Revelation, we are told of God's plan to one day restore His creation to perfection.

Right now, Jesus sits on His throne in heaven, but at the appointed time, He will come back for His people. All things will be made new. Light will pierce the darkness. Praises will resound throughout the earth. Revelation 21:3–4 describes the new creation in this way: "Look, God's dwelling is with humanity, and he will live with them. They will be his peoples, and God himself will be with them and will be their God. He will wipe away every tear from their eyes. Death will be no more; grief, crying, and pain will be no more, because the previous things have passed away." No longer will Satan roam to and fro on the earth. God's children will finally rest in His presence. Jesus, King of kings and Lord of lords, will take His reign. Oh, how we look forward to that glorious day!

> JESUS SITS ON HIS THRONE IN HEAVEN, BUT AT THE APPOINTED TIME, HE WILL COME BACK FOR HIS PEOPLE.

1. What do we learn about God from these verses?

2. What do we learn about Satan in these verses?

3. Even though God allows suffering, why can we trust Him?

ATTRIBUTE OF GOD I'M MEDITATING ON TODAY

REMEMBER THIS

Job's Suffering

Do you ever think in worst-case scenarios? If so, you are not alone. In preparation for future events, our anxious minds often ask, *What if?* We plot our tactics in preparation for every possible outcome. And somehow, the forethought gives us an illusion of peace. Rarely do our wildest "what ifs" become our reality. Rarely do we have to face the fears we dream up in our minds. But Job did.

In today's readings, Job faces unimaginable tragedies. Reading these events on a page does not give them the color they deserve. As we ponder these verses, let us place ourselves in Job's shoes. What was a seemingly normal, leisurely day turned into wave after wave of heartache. We know the feeling, right? The normalcy we rest in can change with one phone call, one glance away from the road, one slam of the door. Sometimes aching hearts break gradually; sometimes, they shatter in an instant.

In Job's story, his heart shattered. First, a messenger rushes to inform Job that foreign travelers have attacked his oxen, donkeys, and servants. His property has been stolen, and his beloved servants have been murdered. Anyone who has faced an act of robbery knows this feeling all too well. All of a sudden, your comfort is disrupted with the reminder: this world is not safe. Before Job can process the theft, another messenger appears. This time, Job is informed that lightning came down and struck his sheep and the servants who tended to them. This tragedy speaks to the loss we experience from natural disasters. Hurricanes, tornadoes, tsunamis, snowstorms, forest fires, earthquakes, and more all wreak havoc on our homes without apology. Natural disasters remind us of our lack of control. At just a moment's notice, Job's security is shaken. Again, a messenger comes and reports more horrible news. Job's estate has again fallen prey to foreign invaders. This time, his camels were besieged, and his servants were murdered. These animals and servants represent Job's wealth accumulated throughout his life, possibly even an inheritance passed on through generations. Once the greatest man in the kingdom (Job 1:3), Job now has little to his name.

Job reminds us that God is still God, even when chaos ensues.

WEEK ONE | DAY FOUR

These tragedies pale in comparison to the next one. Another messenger comes to deliver the most horrific news yet. A mighty wind swept over his eldest son's house, collapsing it on all of his children. Job's pride and joy, his namesakes, his beloved family — all crushed under a single gush of wind. This kind of wound cuts deeper than the others. Many share in the grief of losing a son or daughter, the gaping hole dug in one's heart that never seems to fully heal. Job experienced this hurt multiplied by ten. Each one of his seven sons and three daughters died together that day. Just a few hours earlier, Job was relishing in the goodness of God. Suddenly, he is confronted with the brokenness all around him.

How does Job respond? In verse 20, we see Job shave his head and tear his clothes, common signs of mourning and great distress in the Old Testament. These actions clue us in to the heart-wrenching pain that Job is experiencing. Yet, even in the depth of mourning, Job's response is to praise God. In Job 1:21, we see Job's first words after the loss of his wealth and his children. Job likely feels exposed, vulnerable, and unbearably sad, yet he says, "The LORD gives, and the LORD takes away. Blessed be the name of the LORD." Even in the middle of grief, Job recognizes the sovereignty of God. God's sovereignty means that He holds all power, all authority, and all control in the grand vastness of the universe and in the everyday details of our lives. Even in tragedy, Job holds on to what he knows is true of God.

In these verses, Job introduces us to a biblical language called lament. Lament is the language of the sufferer, prayers prayed in times of mourning, fear, or loss that grieve a broken world. But lament is much more than sorrow; it is a choice to trust God no matter the circumstance. Lament is laying our darkest emotions before God and trusting that He is faithful and in control. In fact, over a third of the psalms are songs of lament, giving us words to pray in our darkest times.

Job's response in Job 1:21–22 is a prayer of deep hurt and deep reverence — proof that we can hold conflicting emotions together in our hands. Job provides us with encouragement in times of suffering. In our lowest lows, when we fear we may shatter with just one more blow, the presence of God lifts our eyes. If every penny we own is stolen, if every family member of ours passes away, if every friend betrays us — God still sits on the throne in heaven.

Even more, through His Son, Jesus, God left His throne, took on flesh, and suffered on our behalf. Philippians 2:6–8 says it best: "[Jesus] existing in the form of God, did not consider equality with God as something to be exploited. Instead he emptied himself by assuming the form of a servant, taking on the likeness of humanity. And when he had come as a man, he humbled himself by becoming obedient to the point of death — even to death on a cross." Our gracious God experienced our suffering — our everyday pains and the deepest of tragedy. He felt thorns in His feet, the sting of sunburn, and the burn of sweat-drenched wounds. He also felt rejection, betrayal, loss, humiliation, and the greatest pain of all — separation from God, His Father. On the cross, Jesus took on the punishment of our sin, death and separation from God, so that we may be reconciled to the Father. Our limited minds have a hard time comprehending this type of sacrifice. Though His separation from God was temporary, it represents the unfathomable love Jesus has for His Church. Of course, Jesus is called Immanuel or "God With Us," for He truly understands even the deepest hurt.

Though Job did not know the beautiful, redemptive story that would one day unfold through Christ Jesus, he did know that God was worthy of all praise and glory, even in his pain. Job reminds us that God is still God, even when chaos ensues. We can lay our fears, our worries, our disappointments, and even our anger at the feet of Jesus, knowing that He has been there, and He conquered it all. We do not have to hide our feelings from God. We do not have to put on a happy face. We can cry out to the One who is sure to hear us.

1. Reflect on Job's loss. Have you ever had a "what if" scenario become a reality? How did you respond?

2. How does Jesus comfort us in our suffering?

3. Read Psalm 6, a psalm of lament. What stands out to you? How does this psalm encourage us to go to the Lord in our despair?

ATTRIBUTE OF GOD I'M MEDITATING ON TODAY

REMEMBER THIS

Psalms of Lament

The Bible never shies away from discussing the brokenness of this world—and the psalms are a testament to this. Throughout the psalms, we frequently see David and other psalmists express their fear, weariness, grief, and deep pain. When we see these feelings expressed in the psalms, we call them psalms of lament.

As believers, we surely experience hardship over and over again throughout our lives. Lament is the language that God's Word gives us to mourn, work through our pain, and ultimately reach healing. Through lament, we can express our deepest hurts while also remembering what is true about God's character. Lament reminds us that we can hold hurt and hope in our hands at the same time. Jesus is the comforter of our hurting hearts. His death and resurrection secured for us a place in the family of God. This means that we can come before God's throne as a child would come before his father—fully heard and fully loved. Read Psalm 6, and notice the feelings that David presents to God but also the deep trust that his cries are heard.

As you read, consider Mark Vroegop's four elements of lament from his book *Dark Clouds, Deep Mercy: Discovering the Grace of Lament*. First, lament begins with addressing God. Though this may seem simple, this is a choice to leave your own solitude and talk to God about your pain. Just as getting out of bed may be the most difficult part of a morning routine, just taking the step to approach God can sometimes be the most difficult aspect of lament.

The second element of lament is bringing your frustrations, complaints, pains, and heartaches to God. This conversation is not sugar-coated but is honest and sincere, trusting that God cares for you and hears you in your hurting.

The third element of lament is seeking God's help and guidance. This is founded on faith, remembering that the God who sent Jesus to die for our sins also will deliver us from our pain. Scripture tells us that God works all things together for His glory and our good (Romans 8:28–30). We can submit to God's control, knowing that He will take every tragedy, every heartache, and every diagnosis and wield it for our ultimate good. He is the God who makes beauty from ashes and rainbows from storms.

The final element of lament is also the goal of lament—the choice to trust God. The ability to trust God with our sufferings strengthens our faith, for we get a deeper understanding of God's character. He is Immanuel. He is God with us—in every tear and in every fear.

Instructions

Highlight the psalm on the following page based on the four elements of lament.

HIGHLIGHT IN GREEN:

Choices made to address God or present suffering to God.

HIGHLIGHT IN ORANGE:

Complaints, frustrations, fears, etc., that the author brings before God's throne.

HIGHLIGHT IN BLUE:

Requests for God's help and guidance.

HIGHLIGHT IN YELLOW:

Statements that reveal a decision to trust God.

Psalm 6

Lord, do not rebuke me in your anger;

do not discipline me in your wrath.

Be gracious to me, Lord, for I am weak;

heal me, Lord, for my bones are shaking;

my whole being is shaken with terror.

And you, Lord — how long?

Turn, Lord! Rescue me;

save me because of your faithful love.

For there is no remembrance of you in death;

who can thank you in Sheol?

I am weary from my groaning;

with my tears I dampen my bed

and drench my couch every night.

My eyes are swollen from grief;

they grow old because of all my enemies.

Depart from me, all evildoers,

for the Lord has heard the sound of my weeping.

The Lord has heard my plea for help;

the Lord accepts my prayer.

All my enemies will be ashamed and shake with terror;

they will turn back and suddenly be disgraced.

More Psalms of Lament* to Consider

PSALM 4   PSALM 40

PSALM 5   PSALM 42

PSALM 10   PSALM 55

PSALM 13   PSALM 56

PSALM 17   PSALM 69

PSALM 22   PSALM 70

PSALM 27   PSALM 77

PSALM 28   PSALM 86

PSALM 31   PSALM 142

*Note: This list is not exhaustive.

Job's Second Test

Riptides—the unstoppable, invisible force beneath crashing waves—are usually strongest when a storm is present. These currents will pick you up, sweep you under, and carry you out to sea—threatening the life of even the strongest swimmers. The best advice for those facing riptides is simply this: do not get in the water. But what if you have no choice? What if you are thrown into the water against your will? Today, we will see Job facing riptides of incomparable strength. We will see him in desperation, intensely treading water and trying to stay afloat amidst another attack from Satan.

We again become flies on the wall in the throneroom of heaven. In many ways, this scene mirrors the one prior. God holds a meeting with His heavenly council, and Satan presents himself before the Lord, likely fuming in frustration at Job's loyalty. Again, Satan reports that he has been roaming around the earth. He sounds like a teenager giving the bare minimum to a parent's question—evasive and sneaky. Yet God again proposes His servant Job, the man of integrity. Though God had partially removed His protective hedge from around Job and his family, Job did not curse God (Job 1:10; 2:6). In verse 3, we see Satan's true goal. He wants to destroy Job, the lover of God. Perhaps he feels threatened by Job's unwavering loyalty.

And so, Satan asks for another shot, wishing to test Job once more. He proposes that Job's suffering has not cut deep enough. So far, Satan has attacked Job's possessions and children—external belongings. Satan wants to make his attack personal. He wants to strike Job's flesh in torture, even while Job is grieving for his family. God allows this second test but again sets boundaries for Satan. In Job 1:12, God gave Satan access to everything Job owned, now in Job 2:6, God expands that boundary. Satan's only restriction now is that he is not allowed to take Job's life.

This poor man has had almost everything taken from him—his wealth, his servants, and his children. Why would God allow him to suffer futher? This mystery is

God is worthy of our praise from now to the end of our days.

WEEK ONE | DAY FIVE

perplexing. God Himself called Job "a man of perfect integrity" (Job 1:8, 2:3). He is already barely treading water, so why whisk him out to sea? We never get a formal answer. Perhaps God will not settle for partial glory. He wants and deserves to be glorified in all circumstances. Even in the midst of agonizing pain—emotionally and physically—He wants our praise, for He is worthy. Though Job will suffer greater, God sees future triumph on the other side. Perhaps this riptide will carry him somewhere better.

Again Satan leaves God's presence to attack Job. This time, we do not see outside forces attacking Job as in previous tests. The very hand of Satan infects boils that cover Job's body from the crown of his head to the tips of his toes. In Job 7:5, we read more descriptions of Job's sores: they are open, festering, and filled with maggots. He uses broken pieces of pottery to relieve the itch of his broken body. His salty tears sting his cheeks.

In every sense of the word, Job is exposed. Job finds a new home among the ashes. In ancient times, "the ashes" referred to the designated place outside the city walls where trash and human waste were piled to be burned. Job was once the greatest man in his region (Job 1:3), highly praised and highly honored. Now he has lost everything and is an outcast, only welcome in the most detestable of places, a hell on earth of sorts. His body is constantly burning, constantly reminding him of his loss.

Job's wife feeds his agony. She tempts him with the easy way out—to let the riptide sweep him under, cursing God into his death. Satan's temptations are often the easier option, are they not? This is exactly what Satan wants—for Job to be destroyed and the light of God to be ever-so-slightly dimmed. He knows God's love for His children, and by attacking Job, Satan attacks God. But still, though water figuratively fills his lungs and breath escapes him, Job keeps treading. He does not curse God with his lips. Though the rest of the book will show Job's struggle to reconcile the goodness of God with his present circumstances, Job 2:10 tells us that Satan lost the challenge. Job did not give in. He did not dishonor God.

Today, we may ask, *Where is Jesus amidst such suffering? Where is the gospel in such pain?* Skin diseases like Job's were seen as a sign of sure rebellion from God. Like a scarlet letter, the boils were a shame-evoking symbol of disobedience, banishing Job to the margins of his community. Yet throughout the gospels, we see Jesus not only conversing with those who have such diseases—the lepers, the diseased, and the broken—but we see Him reach out His hand to touch them (Matthew 8:3). The most loathsome people are the ones upon whom Jesus placed His hand. Can you imagine that moment? Likely, these people had not been touched by another person for months, if not years. But Jesus restored their worth by healing their bodies and their spirits.

On this side of the cross, we have the privilege of reading stories of Jesus's healing hand, His intentional conversations, and His promise of a kingdom that knows no suffering. But Job did not have these stories. He may not have known any of God's covenant promises of love and faithfulness to His children. Even so, he trusted the God he communed with over and over throughout the earlier days of his life. Job is an example to us all. Even if we did not have the cross, even if we can see no end to the darkness, even if we drown beneath the current, God is worthy of our praise from now to the end of our days.

> JOB 2:10 TELLS US THAT SATAN LOST THE CHALLENGE. JOB DID NOT GIVE IN. HE DID NOT DISHONOR GOD.

1. Though we are not formally given an answer, why do you think God allows Satan to test Job?

2. Ponder Job's suffering. Have you ever felt overcome with pain? How does this help you empathize with Job?

ATTRIBUTE OF GOD I'M MEDITATING ON TODAY

REMEMBER THIS

Think back on all of the Scripture that you read and studied
this week as you answer the questions below.

What did you observe about God and His character?

What did you learn about the condition of mankind and yourself?

How does this week's Scripture point to the gospel?

How do the truths you have learned this week about God, man,
and the gospel give you hope, peace, or encouragement?

How should you respond to what you read and learned this week?
Write down one or two specific action steps you can take this week to apply what you learned.
Then, write a prayer in response to your study of God's Word.

Before we begin a new week of study, take some time to apply and share the truths of Scripture you learned this week. Here are a few ideas of how you could do this:

1. Schedule a meet-up with a friend to share what you are learning from God's Word.

2. Use these prompts to journal or pray through what God is revealing to you through your study of His Word.

   a. Lord, I feel…

   _____

   _____

   _____

   _____

   b. Lord, You are…

   _____

   _____

   _____

   _____

   c. Lord, forgive me for…

   _____

   _____

   _____

   _____

d. Lord, help me with…

_____

_____

_____

_____

3. Spend time worshiping God in a way that is meaningful to you, whether that is taking a walk in nature, painting, drawing, singing, etc.

4. Paraphrase the Scripture you read this week.

_____

_____

_____

_____

_____

_____

_____

5. Use a study Bible or commentary to help you answer questions that came up as you read this week's Scripture.

6. Take steps to fulfill the action steps you listed on Day 5.

7. Use highlighters to mark the places you see the metanarrative of Scripture in one or more of the passages that you read this week.
    (See the Metanarrative of Scripture on page 14.)

Scripture Memory

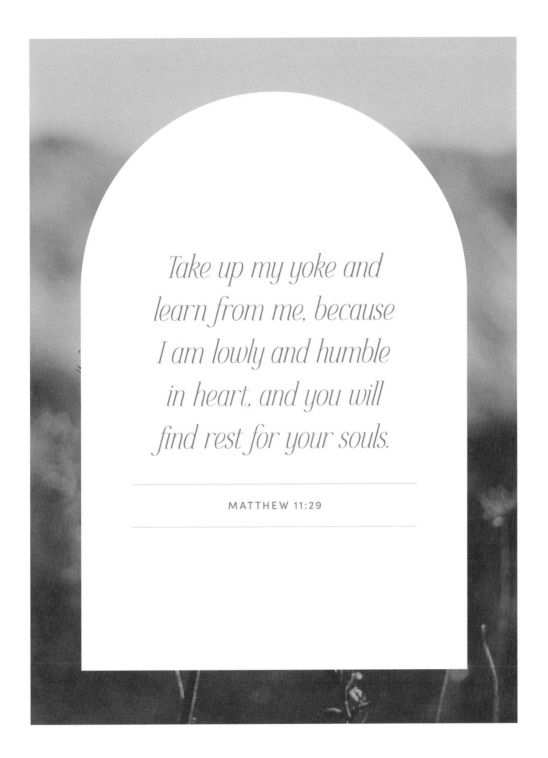

Take up my yoke and learn from me, because I am lowly and humble in heart, and you will find rest for your souls.

MATTHEW 11:29

The Friends of the Sufferer

PRACTICE THIS WEEK'S MEMORY VERSE + READ JOB 2:11–13

Place yourself in Job's shoes. You sit among the ashes of burned rubbish. The putrid smells that were once overwhelming now do not phase you — they are your new normal. Your heart aches for your children. Your body burns in pain. Near the brink of death, life seems to have no point. You can see your city in the distance — it bustles with everyday prosperity, mocking your current home in the wasteland. You cannot utter words, for there are no words to describe the depth of your agony. Covered in dust, you stare into the distance, praying this is just a nightmare.

As awful as this sounds, Job's reality was likely much worse. In today's reading, we see three friends who journeyed together to visit Job, and they found his condition more despairing than they could have imagined. Alone and disfigured, Job was barely recognizable. The life and vibrance must have been zapped from him. Job was empty, merely a shell of a human. And so, these friends tore their clothes and joined Job in his despair. Together, they sat upon the ashes for seven days and seven nights, weeping aloud. These were tears that expressed genuine care and authentic mourning alongside their friend. No one uttered a word. In the depth of their souls, they had to know no words could suffice.

Who were these friends? Where did they come from? Scripture names each of them — Eliphaz the Temanite, Bildad the Shuhite, and Zophar the Naamathite. They came from different countries with different upbringings, but these friends were united in sympathy for their friend Job. When the friends heard of Job's tragedies, they coordinated a time to visit him. Because we know they did not live nearby, this visit likely occurred weeks or months after Satan struck Job. Think about it — that means Job sat in the ashes, alone and in silence, for days upon days.

The cold ache of grief finds tender warmth in Jesus's presence.

WEEK TWO | DAY ONE

In these few verses, Job's friends set a profound example of how we should care for our mourning friends. They left their comfort and convenience, coordinated amongst each other, traveled several days to Uz, and joined Job in the most detestable part of town. Remember, Job was diseased and in constant pain. His home, his wife, and his everyday conveniences brought him no comfort. The pit of ash seemed the only fitting setting to match his pain. We do not see townspeople or neighbors joining Job in compassion; only these three friends came near. They did what others would not do. They came close to Job in his time of need when others chose to keep their distance.

As we read through the rest of Job, the compassion of these friends will fade into cruelty. Chapters 4–37 will consist of an ongoing discourse between Job and his visitors, in which they attempt to reason and explain away Job's sufferings. Their words will cut deeper than the sores that cover his body. But for now, we must remember that their intentions started with care and love for their dear friend.

Perhaps we are led to ask the question: What would Jesus say to Job's suffering? Would He ever break the silence? In Jesus's famous speech, the Sermon on the Mount (Matthew 5–7), Jesus describes His coming kingdom, and it looks much different from what one may expect. The Beatitudes, which serve as the opening for the Sermon on the Mount, tell us that the kingdom of God does not favor the famous or the powerful, but instead, it lifts up the poor in spirit, the humble, and the persecuted (Matthew 5:3–10). Jesus pronounces a specific blessing over those who mourn, promising that they will be comforted (Matthew 5:4). The cold ache of grief finds tender warmth in Jesus's presence.

Job has much to grieve over—his family, his wealth, his dreams for the future, and his current pain. But the Beatitudes remind us that Christ alone is the solace and the security Job needs. Jesus sees, hears, and knows the trials that each one of us faces. And in the Beatitudes, these struggles are recognized and rewarded for those who are in Christ. What's more, in Isaiah 9:6, Jesus is called "Wonderful Counselor, Mighty God, Eternal Father, Prince of

Peace." Jesus is the One we need in our pain because His perspective is not limited like ours. He counsels us with the end in mind—an end that displays the might of God and the peace that will one day rule the earth. This end is more splendid and beautiful than we can imagine. Likely, Jesus would encourage Job to keep his eyes locked on the splendor of eternity that awaits him in heaven. Even if Job cannot see redemption for his tragedies on earth, his pain will one day dissipate in the glory and radiance of Jesus. His questions will be answered (1 Corinthians 13:12). Job's soul will finally rest.

In the coming weeks, we will observe how Job's friends comforted him with a narrow, finite perspective. Seven days and seven nights of mourning, ripping clothes, and sitting in ashes were customary signs of respectful grief in ancient times. Yes, the friends went above and beyond in their travels to care for Job, but the depths of their compassion were limited because they were limited human beings. They only did what they knew to do. Jesus knows deeper. Jesus knows every corner of our souls and all of our hiding places. Jesus knows eternity past and eternity future. Jesus invites us to accept His limitless comfort that promises help for today and hope for tomorrow.

With Jesus as our example, we can grow in our love and care for our suffering neighbors. Who in our circle is in a season of despair? Who feels as if they are an outcast? Who has been tumbled under wave after wave of heartache? As followers of Christ, we are empowered with His very Spirit to be the gentle friend who listens well, talks less, and leaves our comfort to care for the broken.

We may not have the right words to say. We may feel ill-equipped. We may have a hard time navigating needs. We may even feel intimidated by the sheer depth of their mourning. But we can show up. We can pray for words; we can share Scripture; we can fold laundry, cook dinners, call to check in, and above all, we can be a listening ear. When we are tempted to fill empty space with seemingly wise words, let us lean into silent compassion. Just as Job's friends did, we can lay down our pride and sit in the ashes with our brothers and sisters. Let us be known by our love (John 13:35).

1. What did Job's friends get right in their care for Job?

2. Why are healthy Christian relationships important in times of suffering?

3. Who do you know that is currently in a season of suffering?
   What practical things can you do to show them the love of Jesus?

ATTRIBUTE OF GOD I'M MEDITATING ON TODAY

REMEMBER THIS

Job's Comforters

ELIPHAZ

From: Teman in Edom

3 Speeches: Chapters 4–5, 15, 22

A Sage Who Lost His Temper

Wise, quick-tempered, long-winded

BILDAD

From: Shuah (Arabia)

3 Speeches: Chapters 8, 18, 25

The Keeper of Tradition

Orthodox, militant, concise

ZOPHAR

From: Na'amah (Arabia)

2 Speeches: Chapters 11, 20

The Quick-Witted Accuser

Sarcastic, impatient, intolerant

"But humans are born for trouble as surely as sparks fly upward."

ELIPHAZ, JOB 5:7

"If you are pure and upright, then he will move even now on your behalf and restore the home where your righteousness dwells."

BILDAD, JOB 8:6

"But a stupid person will gain understanding as soon as a wild donkey is born a human!"

ZOPHAR, JOB 11:12

Job's Lament

Did you keep a diary or a journal growing up? If so, the pages were likely filled with words you did not tell anyone else. You may have written in a stream of consciousness—your thoughts flowing seamlessly onto paper. The grammar may have been incorrect; there may have been scribbled words and chicken-scratch handwriting, but these journal entries are authentic. They showed your truest, most real thoughts. Today, we enter into Job's mind in the midst of his darkest days. Just like our diaries and journals, chapter 3 is authentic and raw—and perhaps the most haunting chapter in all of Job.

Job himself breaks the seven-day, seven-night silence. But his speech is not conversational. He does not seem to be talking to his friends or even to God. Instead, it is as if Job monologues his innermost thoughts. Job does not ask for a response, and his questions are rhetorical. He simply voices his thoughts.

If we had to pick one word to describe Job's heart after reading chapter 3, a great choice would be "unrest." Job is wrestling with his current circumstances and the gracious God he has spent his life serving. Job's heart is like a boat, tossed and battered by winds, directionless after a storm.

First, in verses 1–12, Job curses his birth. As he processes his trauma, he questions not just his current circumstances but the very reason for his existence. He wishes darkness upon his day of birth—that he would have arrived stillborn. He wishes darkness even on the day of his conception, somehow wishing his parents would have never even come together to form him. By escaping conception and birth, Job would never have experienced anything good—or anything hurtful. Ultimately, he is asking the question: *Why do I exist in the first place?*

Job continues his lament by wishing to rest with the dead. In verses 13–22, Job moves outside of his personal hurt and extends it onto all of humanity. Why are those who search diligently for death even given life at the start? He describes kings and rulers who

The Christian life is a life of mourning brokenness and anticipating the full and final hope of Jesus's return.

WEEK TWO | DAY TWO

reign in power but end up buried among the dead, just as their subjects do. He finds himself relating to a slave who longs for the grave as an end to his oppression. Death is the only sigh of relief that Job can imagine in the midst of his continuous afflictions. Job lived year after year in the peace and provision of God, serving Him mightily and being a beacon of righteousness in his community. Now, Job wishes for an end to the turmoil, the type of rest that comes from death.

Job's words are heavy and dark—they sting with sadness and ache with extinguished hope. In the deepest crevices of Job's heart, he longs for peace to return to his soul. At the very core of who we are, when everything is stripped away and our bodies fail us, we long for rest. This rest is escaping Job as he attempts to navigate through the pains, the groanings, and the realized nightmares. As he sits upon the trash heap, Job mourns the life he knew. In the coming chapters, Job will ask big questions of God and beg for God's presence. We will see Job fight for understanding and peace to be reinstated in his heart. But for now, he sits lonely in the ashes, filled with questions with few answers. At this time, Job's sadness clouds his ability to see God's care for him.

The beauty of the gospel is that we have a fellow sufferer in Jesus—One who knows the feeling of being humiliated on the cross. Similarly to Job's anguish, Jesus asked, "My God, my God, why have you abandoned me?" (Matthew 27:46). Isaiah 53:3 describes Jesus as "a man of suffering who knew what sickness was." In the New Testament, we see Jesus's experiences with pain and grief. We see Jesus in mourning following the death of His friend Lazarus, joining Lazarus's family in tears (John 11). Though Jesus was about to raise His friend from the dead, He still shed tears, perhaps exhibiting His humble and lowly heart, joining the hurt of the mourners.

Unlike Job, Jesus knew the coming joy awaiting Him in heaven after His suffering. Job did not yet know God's unfolding redemptive story, but through Jesus, God answers Job's burning questions. The greatest sufferer became the greatest Savior. For us today, suffering holds great meaning and communion with

Jesus, as we lean into His strength with the knowledge that He has secured great hope for us in and through our trials.

Just as Jesus wept with those mourning Lazarus, Job's story offers us a chance to grieve with him. As followers of Christ, we are called to "weep with those who weep" (Romans 12:15). Today, we are to solemnly humble ourselves—forgetting our cheerful mornings, fresh coffee, or dinner plans—and mourn alongside our friend Job as his soul is crushed to the point of desiring death. We are to sit in stillness with the hurting. Job does not need wise words from friends, which will soon come. He needs God. Is that not what we all need?

As we listen to Job's lament, we can consider our care for those mourning around us and take the temperature of our hearts toward our suffering neighbors. Do our eyes fill with tears alongside them? Do we rest in silence with the sufferer? Job's experience should cause us to slow down, remember the feelings of agony and despair, and mourn that others have to experience that same pain. In the wake of tragedies in our communities and around the world, do we sit in grief with those who suffer, or do we move along with our day? The Christian life is not one of consistent okay-ness; the Christian life is a life of mourning brokenness and anticipating the full and final hope of Jesus's return.

> FOR US TODAY, SUFFERING HOLDS GREAT MEANING AND COMMUNION WITH JESUS.

1. What words would you use to describe Job's current condition after reading Job 3?

2. What did you learn about Jesus and His heart toward the sufferer from today's study?

3. What is your typical response to those in a season of suffering? How can you grow in your care?

ATTRIBUTE OF GOD I'M MEDITATING ON TODAY

REMEMBER THIS

Jesus in Our Suffering

The book of Job is a story of an innocent man, fully devoted to God, who experiences and perseveres through insurmountable suffering to prove that God's glory triumphs over darkness. Does this sound familiar? Hundreds of years after Job lived, Jesus Christ also suffered deeply through His death on the cross, though He was innocent. Yet Jesus rose from the dead to prove that God is victorious over evil. The story of Job whets our appetites in longing and expectation for the Savior to come, Jesus Christ. Job is ultimately a story about Jesus.

"

The story of Job whets our appetites in longing and expectation for the Savior to come, Jesus Christ.

Who is Jesus in the midst of our suffering?

OUR COMFORTER *2 Corinthians 1:3–4*	**OUR SUFFICIENCY** *2 Corinthians 12:9*
OUR REFUGE *Psalm 18:2*	**OUR FELLOW SUFFERER** *Isaiah 53:3*
OUR FRIEND *John 15:15*	**OUR PEACE** *Ephesians 2:14–18*
OUR HOPE *Revelation 21:5–7*	**OUR REST** *Matthew 11:28–30*
OUR TRIUMPH *John 16:33*	**OUR STRENGTH** *1 Peter 5:10*
OUR COUNSELOR *John 14:26*	**OUR TRUTH** *John 14:6*

OUR REDEMPTION
Ephesians 1:7–8

Eliphaz's First Speech

Today, we read the first discourse between Eliphaz and Job. This speech begins a series of speeches that are found in Job between chapters 4 and 37, making up the body, or the middle, of Job. There are three rounds of speeches, each with a series of back-and-forth discourse between Job and his friends (see the outline of Job on page 17). Though Job's friends begin speaking with good intentions, they spiral into impatience for Job's misery.

Throughout these speeches, Eliphaz, Bildad, and Zophar attempt to apply reason to Job's suffering. Their words are wise by the world's standards but often fail in gentleness — throwing salt into Job's open wounds. For the next couple of weeks, the reading for each day of this study will be longer, covering three to five chapters of Job. Hang in there with us! These chapters will help us navigate our own theology of suffering and expand our view of God. The word "theology" may seem complex, but it simply refers to the study of God; our theology is what we believe to be true about God. As Job tries to reconcile his theological beliefs with his lived experience, we will see Job continue to pursue the Lord wholeheartedly, even in the midst of his unrest. By the end of Job, we will gain a fresh reverence of God that strengthens our faith and reminds us of His goodness during any and all seasons of our lives.

Returning to our discussion about Job and his friends, we see that we do not have genealogies or backgrounds of Job, Eliphaz, Bildad, or Zophar. However, we do know where each friend is generally from (see the map on pages 26–27), which provides some insight into their lives and the perspectives they bring into their speeches. Eliphaz is perhaps the kindest, most considerate of the friend trio. He is from a place called Teman in Edom, a place known for its depth of wisdom. Likely, Eliphaz is a thought leader in Teman, as he speaks with both eloquence and confidence.

Every longing in our hearts is a longing for Jesus.

WEEK TWO | DAY THREE

Eliphaz begins his speech in thoughtfulness, asking Job for a chance to speak. Remember, Eliphaz, Bildad, and Zophar mourned with Job for the customary amount of time, yet Job's lament reflects a deeply burdened heart. In an effort to help pull him out of the ashes, Eliphaz kindly pleads with Job to remember what they both believe to be true about God. He reminds Job of his past, crediting him with instructing many in wisdom and with upholding the weak. Eliphaz seems to say: *Job, you have served God well throughout your days—will He not redeem you from this horror?* Eliphaz's theology supports that God upholds and protects the righteous but punishes the wicked (Job 4:7)—and, as we see from Job's responses, this seems to have been Job's theological framework as well. However, Job's former theology is currently shaken. In the middle of his suffering, Job is still wrestling with his faith, and so an appeal to Job's former beliefs is irrelevant. Job's understanding of God is being reshaped.

Eliphaz continues his speech with an odd dream. In his sleep, he sees a dark, ominous spirit who says to him, "Can a mortal be righteous before God? Can a man be more pure than his Maker?" (Job 4:17). This experience informs the rest of his speech, as he reminds Job that no man could possibly be perfect before God's holy throne. Eliphaz encourages Job to seek God and repent of the sins he has committed. If Job would repent of his sin, Eliphaz believes that God would restore what Job has lost. Eliphaz's speech encourages Job to get up, shake off the dust of loss, and apologize to God.

On the surface, many of Eliphaz's observations are biblically sound. In light of eternity, God will one day destroy the wicked and preserve the righteous. Just as Job and Eliphaz believe, God is just. However, God's justice may not be as simple and linear as Eliphaz assumes. Job is in the middle of experiencing the complexity of God, and this "return to your former way of life" exhortation feels shallow.

In Job's response to Eliphaz, he attempts to bring Eliphaz and his friends into understanding, but again, Job is reminded that he is alone. Though his friends sit beside him, they are miles away in their sympathy. Job describes his grief as outweighing the sand of the seas (Job 6:2–3). He accuses God of striking him with arrows and wishes

for God to finally crush him. Job wishes some kind of peace for his tormented soul, and he sees peace in death. Though Eliphaz encourages him to seek redemption, Job scoffs at the suggestion. How can he see hope in the future when he is not sure if he can make it to nightfall?

Finally, Job appeals to God for answers. He is upset with Eliphaz for assuming that he deserves discipline. Job knows deep in his heart that he took great care to follow the instructions of the Lord. Job's experience and his innocence challenge the black-and-white view of God that Eliphaz presents. Job begins to realize that God is much more complex than he previously understood. In Job 7:17–21, Job makes an appeal to God, begging for a reason behind his suffering. Job knows that Eliphaz, Bildad, and Zophar do not hold the answers he needs—only God does.

In these chapters, we learn that every longing in our hearts is a longing for Jesus. Job wishes for someone to understand the weight of his suffering. Jesus, too, suffered intensely. Job longs to be counted righteous. Jesus's sacrifice puts us in righteous standing before God, for our sins are washed clean by His blood. Job longs for his troubled heart to be stilled, and Jesus is our Prince of Peace who brings that stillness. Job has lost hope for his future, yet Jesus recovers our hope with an invitation into His kingdom. Job longs for an answer from God; Jesus is the final answer—the Light of the World that darkness can never overcome.

Just like Job, at the core of our longings is the desire for the love, acceptance, and mercy found in Christ alone. He is our fellow sufferer, the calmer of our storms, and the true Word of God. When the words of Job's friends fall empty—when our words fall empty—we can remember that Jesus's words never will. When we feel alone and misunderstood, let us be encouraged by Isaiah 43:1: "Now this is what the LORD says—the one who created you, Jacob, and the one who formed you, Israel—'Do not fear, for I have redeemed you; I have called you by your name; you are mine.'" If we trust Jesus as our Lord and Savior, we are redeemed from the dark. God's gift of Jesus is our living proof that He has heard our cries, seen our sufferings, and loved us through our doubts. We are His.

1. How would you summarize Eliphaz's first speech?

2. What about Eliphaz's understanding of God is true? What is incomplete?

3. How does the gospel meet Job's longings?

ATTRIBUTE OF GOD I'M MEDITATING ON TODAY

REMEMBER THIS

Bildad's First Speech

Have you ever observed a trial in a courtroom? Two sides plead their case, and then a jury or a judge decides the fate of the disputing parties. Except in this courtroom, you are the defendant, and the judge is God Almighty. In our reading today, Job longs to stand trial before God. He wants to finally clear his name and prove his innocence. Job wants a verdict of some sort—an answer that will ease his restless mind.

But first, Bildad takes the stand. Bildad is from Shuah, which was located in Arabia. Like Job and Eliphaz, Bildad was also likely a prominent figure in his home region. His speech is short, concise, and much less kind when compared to Eliphaz's speech. In fact, Bildad begins his speech angrily. Bildad asserts that Job's complaints against God are "a blast of wind" or hot air (Job 8:2).

In Bildad's theological framework, God is fair. He is always fair and cannot be unfair. Therefore, the good guys receive blessings, and the bad guys are punished. Equations are simple in Bildad's world. This means that Job must have sinned to deserve such extreme loss. And it is on this foundation that Bildad builds his arguments.

To prove his point, Bildad uses a few illustrations: Job's own children, generations of the past, and plants of the marsh. Surely, Bildad claims, Job's children must have sinned boldly against God to deserve a punishment of death (Job 8:4). But Bildad does not know the daily care Job took to sacrifice on behalf of his children (Job 1:5). In fact, sacrifice has no place in Bildad's theology as the good are rewarded, and the bad suffer consequences. There is no grace and no forgiveness.

Next, Bildad calls to the stand generations of the past (Job 8:8–10). Bildad seeks to use past precedent to understand Job's sufferings. Finally, Bildad describes two types of plants

The peace with God that Job longs for is found in Jesus.

WEEK TWO | DAY FOUR

that thrive in the water of a marsh: papyrus and reeds (Job 8:11–19). Because the soil of a marsh is so drenched, plants attach themselves to any firm surface they can find. Therefore, the strength of their roots depends on what they attach themselves to. **Bildad describes those who forsake God as flimsy papyrus or reeds—inevitably torn from their place and rejected. This is why, Bildad theorizes, Job has suffered so deeply.**

Bildad describes God as merely a scale that weighs good and evil. In Bildad's theology, there is no cross, no death, and no resurrection. A god who is as harsh as Bildad describes has no compassion for sinners. But our God, our gracious Father, became human and walked the same dirt that we tread. He healed the sick, befriended the rejected, and dined with sinners. He even sacrificed Himself to forgive the sins of the world.

Place yourself in Job's shoes at this moment. Bildad's rigid god must feel like sandpaper against the wounds of Job's heart. Job responds to Bildad in chapters 9–10. His response is harshly critical of God, accusing Him of finding joy in the pain inflicted upon mankind. If Job was in a courtroom, these accusations would belittle the very character of God. As we read Job's speeches, we must remember that Job is speaking from a heart that has experienced heartbreaking tragedies. He is desperate to understand his loss. The insults that Job hurls at God are not accurate and do not reflect God's compassion for the sufferer. However, even in Job's pain, he seeks God. Job's mouth is riding a rollercoaster of emotions, but his heart is still firmly planted in love for His Maker.

In his desire for answers, Job imagines a courtroom. He is like a criminal appealing his case before the judge who pronounced him guilty. Job will plead his innocence before God, and maybe, just maybe, his heart will receive the rest he longs for. However, Job doubts God would even listen to him. Job feels far away and distant from God. And even if God did listen, Job feels that the very might of God would trump anything he has to say. Job recognizes his stature before a vast and holy God. He describes being swallowed by God's storm just by voicing his complaint (Job 9:17). How can a man stand before God? Job sees the risk that he takes in bringing his case before God, but he feels desperate. And so Job sees two options—death or being pronounced innocent before God. If he cannot bring his case to God's holy courtroom, Job longs for an end to his life.

In the middle of Job's pain, in the depths of his longing, Job wishes for a mediator. He dreams of someone who could go between him and God—someone who can formally present his argument before God. Job wishes for Jesus. Jesus is our compassionate mediator—God's own Son, whose sinless sacrifice bridges the gap between our unholiness and God's holy throne room. Through Jesus, we are heard and comforted. Jesus is our Savior by whose innocent blood we are counted righteous before God (2 Corinthians 5:21). Job longs for grace to be heard by God. Oh, if only Job knew the cleansing water that would soon wash over God's children! The peace with God that Job longs for is found in Jesus.

In the conversation between Bildad and Job, we see two vastly different perspectives of God. In Bildad's mind, God is merely a judge. His sentences are either innocent or guilty. And in some ways, he is right. God will one day execute full judgment against evil in the world. But Bildad misses the compassionate heart of God that provides fullness of grace to those who believe in His Son, Jesus. To Job, God is fierce and mighty, angry even. But Job continually seeks to be heard by Him. Somehow, someway, Job believes God is approachable. (Spoiler alert: at the end of Job, God declares Job's perception of Him correct, while he declares Eliphaz, Bildad, and Zophar's perceptions incorrect.)

Job's zeal to seek the Lord teaches us that God is honored by our efforts to draw near. Even in our anger, even when our struggles cloud our view of Him, we can come to God with the whole of our hearts. In the grand courtroom of God, those of us who are in Christ have been declared innocent through Jesus's sacrifice. We can now pray directly to God and be heard. We do not have to clean ourselves up. We do not have to doctor our prayers. Our raw, human emotion is welcomed by the God who lovingly "heals the brokenhearted and bandages their wounds" (Psalm 147:3).

1. Describe Bildad's theology. How is it right? How is it wrong?

2. Think back to a difficult season of your life. Did you feel heard by God?

3. If Job was granted a hearing before God's court, what would Jesus's role be?

ATTRIBUTE OF GOD I'M MEDITATING ON TODAY

REMEMBER THIS

Zophar's First Speech

Today's reading, consisting of Zophar's speech and Job's reaction, concludes the first round of speeches in the back-and-forth discourse between Job and his "comforters." Let us pause for a moment and remember that Job and his friends are not aware of the conversations between God and Satan that happened in Job 1–2. None of the men know that God Himself called Job "a man of perfect integrity" (Job 1:8, 2:3). No one perceives that Job's suffering has some sort of deeper meaning or larger significance in the span of God's redemptive history. Job and his friends are attempting to reconcile the facts and feelings laid before them with what they believe to be true about God.

And so, with that in mind, let us meet Zophar. He is from Na'amah, a land in Arabia. While Eliphaz and Bildad have three speeches each in Job, Zophar only has two speeches. In the last round of discourse, Zophar does not participate. Though we do not know the reason why Zophar does not speak again, we do observe an impatient and sarcastic tone in his speeches. Perhaps he simply grows exhausted by Job's continuous lament.

Even as his speech begins, Zophar expresses his frustration toward Job; he feels Job should be rebuked for lashing out at God. From just the first six verses of Zophar's speech, we see that he is the harshest among Job's friends. In Job 11:7–12, Zophar describes God's power, and his descriptions of God seem accurate. And in the right context, they are! God is, in fact, limitless. No one can trump His power. However, though Zophar's descriptions of God are correct, the context used is meant to demean Job. It is as if Zophar took a Bible verse out of context; the verse may be true and right, but the use of the truth is unloving and condescending. Zophar's words remind us to be careful in our handling of God's Word. Our words matter, and even if we speak accurately, we may not reflect God's character if we are not first leading with humility and love.

Zophar ends his speech with an encouragement for Job to repent and turn back to the Lord. However, Zophar's encouragement is laced with deceit. He encourages Job to turn back to God, not for a restored relationship but so that God will restore Job's blessings. Zophar affirms Satan's argument in Job 1—humans only want God for what He gives. Zophar's encouragement is also not applicable to Job. He did not have

There is no time wasted in God's presence.

WEEK TWO | DAY FIVE

any outstanding sin lingering before God when his suffering began — thus, there is no sin he needs to turn from in order for his suffering to end. Zophar's speech widens the gap of understanding between Job and his friends. His friends no longer feel "with" him but against him.

From these feelings of opposition, Job begins his speech. His speech is not pointed toward Zophar specifically but toward all three of his friends and God. Job begins by addressing his friends. Job holds a mirror up in front of their faces and asks, "Would it go well if he examined you?" (Job 13:9a). Here, Job reveals a fallacy that sin creates in the human heart — we are quick to see the splinter in someone else's eye, but we are hard-pressed to acknowledge the beam of wood in our own eyes (Matthew 7:3–5). Job argues that their arrogance stems from a lack of understanding of God. In fact, Job argues that he knows God just as well or better than they do (Job 13:1–5). This desire for God is exactly what propels Job to seek answers so fiercely. And so, Job transitions to speak to God.

Like Zophar, Job uses many descriptions of God throughout His speech. He agrees that God is vast, limitless, and all-powerful, but Job adds another descriptor to the list — dangerous (Job 13:13–15). Job knows that by standing before God's holy throne, Job is risking his life. But Job presses on, for he is desperate to ask God, *Why?* His question echoes our own in times of hardship: *God, why am I suffering? Why do you feel so far away? What did I do to deserve this?*

Job holds seemingly conflicting characteristics of God together: God is both holy, which means He is set apart and cannot be around sin, and He is approachable. How can God be both at the same time? We find our answer in the Bible. In the book of Genesis, Adam and Eve become separated from God because of their sin. As the story of Scripture continues, we later see God set up a system of sacrifices through the Mosaic Law that allows His people to have their sins forgiven so that they can again draw close to Him (Exodus 20, Leviticus 1–7). However, even before this sacrificial system was set in place, we see evidence of godly men offering sacrifices to the Lord (Genesis 4:3–5, 8:20–21, 13:4, 22:13, 31:54, 46:1). This was a way for sinful human beings to be forgiven of their sin, momentarily allowing them to approach a Holy God again. Job, too, made sacrifices for the forgiveness of sin (Job 1:5), and God Himself pronounced Job's integrity (Job 1:8, 2:3).

Job's relationship with God is proven in Job 14:13–17. Here, we see Job long for a resurrection. Job asks God to hide him in death, which would be an end to his pain and suffering. But at the right time, Job longs to rejoin God in a restored relationship. He imagines a scenario where sin would be wiped clean, and he could dwell at peace with his beloved Father.

Job's language is one of an intimate partnership between himself and God. Job 14:15 reads, "You would call, and I would answer you. You would long for the work of your hands." Job wishes for more than his former life to be restored—Job wishes for peace with God. One day, hundreds of years later, Job's longing for a resurrection would be fulfilled by our King and Savior, Jesus Christ. Jesus died as the perfect sacrifice—once for all time—to pay the penalty of our sin forever and welcome all who believe in Him back into God's perfect presence. Through the lens of the gospel, we see that Job's understanding of God is profoundly accurate.

However, let us be reminded that Job is still speaking from a deeply hurt, deeply lonely heart. As we will see in the coming chapters, Job is not yet healed. He still has questions. He still desires answers. But even so, Job's heart is aligned with God. It is here, even when we do not understand and our questions remain unanswered, that we plant our feet upon the rock that never fails us. See, Job's years of serving His God cemented a firm foundation of faith that has held him up throughout the tragedies.

Let us learn from Job in our own seasons of trial. The faith that we are building now—the moments dedicated to prayer, the verses we etch upon our hearts, the time spent in our Bibles—are all being used by God to strengthen our hearts for a day of coming trial. Through this faithful perseverance, we are molded and shaped into the image of Christ. James 1:2–3 tells us, "Consider it a great joy, my brothers and sisters, whenever you experience various trials, because you know that the testing of your faith produces endurance." Keep going. Keep persevering. There is no time wasted in God's presence.

1. Describe Zophar's view of God. How is it right? How is it wrong?

2. Job longs for a resurrection — to be made new before God. For us today, we have the opportunity to be made new by trusting in Jesus Christ. Have you trusted in Christ in this way? If so, how has doing so transformed your life? If not, spend some time journaling about how you, like Job, desire to be made new.

ATTRIBUTE OF GOD I'M MEDITATING ON TODAY

REMEMBER THIS

*Think back on all of the Scripture that you read and studied
this week as you answer the questions below.*

What did you observe about God and His character?

What did you learn about the condition of mankind and yourself?

How does this week's Scripture point to the gospel?

How do the truths you have learned this week about God, man,
and the gospel give you hope, peace, or encouragement?

How should you respond to what you read and learned this week?
Write down one or two specific action steps you can take this week to apply what you learned.
Then, write a prayer in response to your study of God's Word.

Before we begin a new week of study, take some time to apply and share the truths of Scripture you learned this week. Here are a few ideas of how you could do this:

1. Schedule a meet-up with a friend to share what you are learning from God's Word.

2. Use these prompts to journal or pray through what God is revealing to you through your study of His Word.

   a. Lord, I feel…

   _____

   _____

   _____

   _____

   b. Lord, You are…

   _____

   _____

   _____

   _____

   c. Lord, forgive me for…

   _____

   _____

   _____

   _____

d. Lord, help me with…

_____

_____

_____

_____

3. Spend time worshiping God in a way that is meaningful to you, whether that is taking a walk in nature, painting, drawing, singing, etc.

4. Paraphrase the Scripture you read this week.

_____

_____

_____

_____

_____

_____

_____

5. Use a study Bible or commentary to help you answer questions that came up as you read this week's Scripture.

6. Take steps to fulfill the action steps you listed on Day 5.

7. Use highlighters to mark the places you see the metanarrative of Scripture in one or more of the passages that you read this week.
   (See the Metanarrative of Scripture on page 14.)

Scripture Memory

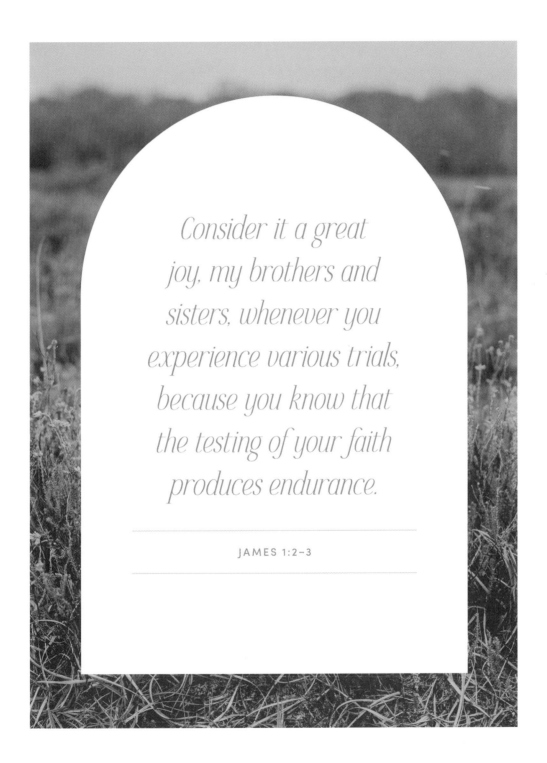

Consider it a great joy, my brothers and sisters, whenever you experience various trials, because you know that the testing of your faith produces endurance.

JAMES 1:2–3

Eliphaz's Second Speech

PRACTICE THIS WEEK'S MEMORY VERSE + READ JOB 15–17

Imagine yourself stuck on the side of a highway. Your tire blows, and you have no idea how to repair it yourself. You begin to panic, but then you remember a trusted friend who you know will come to your rescue. After you thank him, he says, "Oh, it is no trouble. I know you would do the same for me." Underlying this common phrase is the modern moral philosophy: "Good things come to those who do good, and bad things come to those who do bad." Your friend helps because he believes he will one day be helped. This is the foundation of karma—good actions now merit good outcomes in the future. As we observe Job's friends' speeches, we will notice a similar, likely familiar moral philosophy threading throughout their arguments.

Today, we dive into the second round of speeches between Job and his friends. Remember, there are three rounds of speeches in total. Just as Eliphaz began the first round of speeches, now he begins the second. However, the compassionate tone Eliphaz maintained in his first speech is now exchanged for frustration. Though Job longs to be heard by God, Eliphaz believes Job's words are a waste of his breath. According to Eliphaz, Job's determination to be heard by God proves his arrogance. Eliphaz asserts that God does not even think of the heavens as holy, much less a sinful human being (Job 15:14–16). Finally, Eliphaz closes his second speech by essentially communicating the idea that what goes around comes around (Job 15:34–35).

As we continue delving into the speeches between Job and his friends, it is helpful to note that Job's friends hold to retribution theology. Retribution means that God punishes the wicked and rewards the righteous. We see this principle detailed in Deuteronomy 28, as God lovingly describes the blessings to come to Israel if they obey Him and warns of the curses to come if they disobey. And we know this in our own lives;

The only constant in life, the only dependable truth to shape our view of the world, is that God is faithful.

WEEK THREE | DAY ONE

our disobedience has consequences. However, their application of this principle is incorrect. Eliphaz and Job's friends assume that Job must have sinned to experience such terrible suffering.

However, as we look at the world around us today, it does not take long to see that bad things happen to "good" people every day. Suffering is not as simple as Eliphaz proposes. In fact, in John 9, Jesus and His disciples observe a man born blind. The disciples ask Jesus, "Who sinned, this man or his parents, that he was born blind?" Jesus responds that this man's blindness is not a result of the family's disobedience but is so that God's works may be displayed in him (John 9:1–3). So, too, is Job's suffering. Both the blind man's healing and God's coming restoration of Job showcase God's desire to come near to the brokenhearted and bring redemption through tragedy. The only constant in life, the only dependable truth to shape our view of the world, is that God is faithful. As we read about Job's wrestling with his faith, God's faithfulness will be the rock he stands on—the truth that keeps him returning to his God over and over again.

But his wrestling is not always pretty. Job's response to Eliphaz seems eerily similar to his speech that broke the seven-day silence in Job 3. Job's tone is disheartened. Job wishes for comfort—comfort he knows can only come from God. However, Job is now conflicted because he believes that his comforter is also his assailer. Throughout Job 16:6–14, Job accuses God. God has exhausted him, devastated him, shriveled him up, thrown him to the wicked, crushed him, and burst him open. Job—sitting upon a pile of ashes and suffering from painful sores—feels like an enemy of God. Job provides a vivid picture of his grief for us. In his mourning, he covers his raw skin with sackcloth. His face is permanently reddened by tears. His frame is a shadow. Onlookers who formerly looked up to him now spit in his face (Job 17:6–8).

Even still, Job holds tight to his innocence. He alludes to the story of Cain and Abel, where Abel's innocent blood "cries out" to God from the ground (Genesis 4:10). Job seems to think,

Maybe, just maybe, my blood will catch the attention of God (Job 16:18). Job desires justice; he believes his clean hands will prevail. Yet, even in despair, Job clings to faith. Again, Job hopes for a mediator—an advocate who pleads on his behalf before God. Job understands that God will make a way for those who love Him to be heard. And on a quiet night in Bethlehem, hundreds of years later, God's declaration of love burst forth. Jesus, the Son of God, was treated as an enemy of God. Jesus, the King of the world, was treated as a traitor. Jesus, the Good Shepherd, shed His blood like a sacrificial lamb. The perfect man suffered the most. The blameless man carried the blame.

And so, in the depths of his mourning, Job dreams of a Savior (Job 16:18–21). He imagines One who would go before God on his behalf. Job imagines Jesus. This is a profound look into Job's heart, as Job's longing for justice anticipates God's redemptive plan through Jesus. The minutes, the hours, and the days that Job spent following God throughout his life were not wasted. Those minutes, hours, and days built a relationship with God that Job is clinging to in his darkest hours. Though Job's feelings and experience tell him hope is lost, his faith tells him it is not.

Our daily Bible reading and our time spent in prayer are not checkboxes on our to-do list; they are exercises that are building our faith—cultivating our relationship with God—so that one day we may stand firm like Job. As we discussed last week, James 1:2–4 explains it this way: "Consider it a great joy, my brothers and sisters, whenever you experience various trials, because you know that the testing of your faith produces endurance. And let endurance have its full effect, so that you may be mature and complete, lacking nothing." God uses even Satan's most cruel tactics to show us His power. Therefore, just as James instructs, we can count our trials as joy, for we know our victory depends upon God's strength and not our own. And as we depend on God, our faith grows differently than before. It grows stronger—more refined. It is matured, and little by little, we look more like His Son, Jesus.

1. How has Eliphaz's tone changed from his first speech to his second? What does this tell you about the escalation of Job's friends' arguments?

2. What is the danger of believing "good things come to those who do good, and bad things to those who do bad"?

3. Consider your testimony. What experiences in your life have grown your faith stronger? Are these experiences positive or negative by the world's standards? If negative, what does that show you about God's ability to grow your faith in trials?

ATTRIBUTE OF GOD I'M MEDITATING ON TODAY

REMEMBER THIS

How to Read Long Bible Passages

This week, we will be diving into a few long reading days, but be encouraged — the ending of Job is worth persevering through the middle.

By this point in Job, you may feel like the friends are repeating themselves over and over, building upon the same point — that Job has sinned and deserves what he has experienced. You are not wrong! In the Bible, repetition is intentional. Through the ongoing discourse between Job and his friends, we get a deeper look at grief, the questions it causes us to ask, and the worldly misconceptions surrounding suffering.

If we take a moment to reflect upon our own seasons of suffering, we can probably remember a moment when we asked, "How long will this go on, God?" The lack of brevity in the book of Job reminds us that we are not alone in the uncomfortable and messy moments of our grief.

So how do we persevere practically this week while intentionally soaking in Scripture? Check out these tips as you read long Bible passages this week:

1. Pray and remember. Ask God to help you focus! Remember that all of Scripture is profitable for teaching, rebuking, correcting, and training in righteousness (2 Timothy 3:16).

2. Remove distractions. Put your phone on airplane mode, read at a time of day that is least distracting, and set your to-do list aside for focused time in God's Word.

3. Grab a highlighter. Interacting with the text by highlighting or underlining verses that stick out to you is a helpful way to stay engaged. Unsure of what to highlight? Follow this guide or create your own guide! Remember, the Old Testament anticipates Jesus — highlight with this in mind.

    a. **HIGHLIGHT IN ORANGE:**

    Any reference to sin or judgment.

    b. **HIGHLIGHT IN BLUE:**

    Any reference to the redemption of sin.

    c. **HIGHLIGHT IN YELLOW:**

    Any reference to God's character or glory.

4. Write a short summary of what you have just read after each chapter. You can make this as short as a sentence or two — the point is to regurgitate the text so that it will stick in your memory.

5. Use an audio Bible. If you are having trouble focusing on your physical Bible, remember that many apps have audio versions available. This can be a helpful option if you are feeling overwhelmed.

6. Remember, the end is near. Job is a fascinating look at who God is in the midst of our suffering. After this week, we will spend intentional time soaking in God's words as God speaks directly to Job. In these coming speeches, at last, God will answer Job, teach Job about His character, and satisfy Job with His presence.

> WE ARE NOT ALONE IN THE UNCOMFORTABLE AND MESSY MOMENTS OF OUR GRIEF.

Bildad's and Zophar's Second Speeches

PRACTICE THIS WEEK'S MEMORY VERSE + READ JOB 18–21

Throughout the next few days, we will break form from last week's cadence of reading. Today, we will read both Bildad's and Zophar's second speeches, and tomorrow, we will read Eliphaz's and Bildad's third speeches. Take heart! Though we have many chapters of Job left to go, we are inching toward God's response. There, Job's questions will be satisfied in God's presence. Hang in there. The ending is worth the wait.

Bildad's and Zophar's speeches are similar—both are depictions of hell. Together, they agree that this will soon be Job's destination. To the trio of friends, Job is blaspheming God. He is asking—no, begging—the God who created the moon and stars to answer the call of a lowly, sinful human being. To them, Job's pursuit of God neglects God's holiness. Bildad's speech describes the increasing consequences of the wicked man. His lamp is snuffed out; his tent is darkened; his legs become weak; he stumbles into traps set by himself. Terror, calamity, and disaster come after him. And then, "he is driven from light to darkness and chased from the inhabited world" (Job 18:18). Though he does not say so explicitly, it seems that Bildad is insinuating that this describes Job's future fate. There is no grace in Bildad's religious system—Bildad sees no hope for Job.

Zophar's speech is eerily similar, as together, the friends tumble deeper into frustration and impatience. Zophar is exasperated by Job, and perhaps it is because of this frustration that Zophar does not speak again. He does not contribute to the third round of speeches. Zophar's speech describes what awaits the wicked at the end of their life. Their pride will be their demise. They will be forgotten by those they love, and their children will make amends for their mistakes. Zophar delivers a harsh metaphor that paints a mental picture of his argument. The evil man rolls wickedness around in his mouth, and it tastes sweet to him. But what tastes sweet is rejected by his stomach,

Jesus brings us hope.

WEEK THREE | DAY TWO

and he vomits. Zophar concludes that the wicked will not go unpunished. He will reap what he sows. God will get justice. Though Zophar is not wrong, he over-simplifies God. Like Bildad, he leaves out a vital piece of God's plan: the potential for grace and redemption of the sinner.

Job first responds to Bildad with longings that are likely relatable. Job is tired and worn down from arguments, grief, and estrangement from God. And so, with a broken heart, Job says, "I cry out, 'Violence!' but get no response; I call for help, but there is no justice. He has blocked my way so that I cannot pass through; he has veiled my paths with darkness" (Job 19:7–8). Job feels as if God is not listening. Job feels alone in his suffering. His relatives, his friends, his servants, and even his wife refuse his presence. God was supposed to be the One who never left his side. Yet Job sits in the ashes, likely for months after his tragedies, and feels abandoned by God. He feels as if God is not listening or is even ignoring him. Job pleads for mercy, not only from God but from his friends. He longs for some sympathy—some sort of compassion. Job feels alone in his misery.

But as if he's searching for gold in a coal mine, Job continues to dig through the muck of his feelings to find God. Job's desire to meet God is his only comfort. Though he cannot feel Him, though his circumstances tell him otherwise, Job reminds himself of the truth—God has not forsaken him. Job says, "But I know that my Redeemer lives, and at the end he will stand on the dust. Even after my skin has been destroyed, yet I will see God in my flesh. I will see him myself; my eyes will look at him, and not as a stranger. My heart longs within me" (Job 19:25–27).

Often, Job's faith seems like a rollercoaster. Job curses God, and a few verses later, he praises Him. Job's story is a real, intimate observation of grief. Grief feels like being crushed with hopelessness and punished with misery—but that is not the truth. The truth is that God, through His Son's sacrifice for our sin, was crushed for our iniquities and punished so that we may have peace (Isaiah 53:5). Jesus brings us hope. Job sets an example for us that should not be ignored. When our feelings pull us away from God, we can preach the gospel to ourselves and anchor our minds to what is true. Job is right about God. His Redeemer does live. He existed before time. And hundreds of years after Job lived, He made Himself known to all people when He came to the earth as a baby named Jesus.

Job's response to Zophar is an argument of logic (Job 21). Zophar says that the wicked always get punished by God. But Job does not observe the same phenomenon. Job seems to say, *Look around you! The world is filled with evil people receiving all sorts of blessings.* Often, life can feel this way, does it not? You see liars prosper and the corrupt go unpunished. You see the gossip get the promotion. You see the proud get exalted and the lowly humbled further. At this moment in God's story, His justice is not fully delivered. We cannot quite see the fullness of His plans. Though Jesus has defeated sin, God's plan to redeem the world is not yet complete.

Like Job, we see brokenness surrounding us. We know that God hates sin, yet sin seems to run rampant inside our hearts and throughout the world today. Though we do not know the specific date or time that Jesus will return, the Bible does tell us that it will happen. One day, the world will be made new. The injustices that Job experienced and every ounce of evil in the world will be cast into the darkness. Only goodness, mercy, and praise of our Father will remain.

See, Job's friends are right in this way: God can and will punish the wicked. However, His punishment may not come in the way we anticipate or even in this lifetime. Psalm 37:9 describes God's judgment in this way: "For evildoers will be destroyed, but those who put their hope in the LORD will inherit the land." Judgment is not ours to enact or understand. Judgment rests in the sovereign, almighty, fair, and holy hands of God.

1. Read Psalm 37. How does this Psalm shed light on God's justice? What do you learn from it?

2. In Job 19, we see Job reminding himself of the truth of God's character. How have you had to preach the truth of God's Word to yourself in the past?

3. How does God's judgment of evil bring hope to the believer?

ATTRIBUTE OF GOD I'M MEDITATING ON TODAY

REMEMBER THIS

Eliphaz's and Bildad's Final Speeches

PRACTICE THIS WEEK'S MEMORY VERSE + READ JOB 22–26

The climax of a story is the highest point of drama in a narrative—it is the boiling point of tension. The tension between Job and his friends has been steadily rising, and now it is bubbling to a boil. Today marks the last day of reading the discourses between Job and his three friends. These speeches have served as a window into the depths of the heart of a mourning servant of God. Job's friends have shown us how *not* to comfort those in mourning. And today, his friends reach a new low.

So far, Job's friends have made claims that Job has sinned but have not named specific actions. But in Eliphaz's third and final speech, he blatantly accuses Job of specific sins committed against God. Eliphaz blames him for taking advantage of the poor and neglecting the widows and orphans. In Eliphaz's mind, Job has lorded his wealth and power over those on the margins of society. Is Eliphaz correct? Readers of Job have a unique perspective. We have glimpsed into the throne room of God, where God Himself called Job "a man of perfect integrity" (Job 1:8). It seems that Eliphaz has taken the most likely sins possible of a wealthy, influential man of the time and projected them onto Job's life. Eliphaz slanders the man already in pain; he twists the knife in Job's already-wounded soul.

If we are not careful, we can read Job 22 as a righteous warning for Job to keep his distance from evil. To Eliphaz, Job's persistent pursuit of God is heretical, for it discredits God's authority. He instructs Job to repent and submit before the Lord. And though this is generally great advice, it does not apply to Job. We know that he is innocent. Eliphaz's suggestion mimics Zophar's advice in Job 11—repent so that your blessings may return to you. Eliphaz's shallow understanding of God is exactly what Satan wants for believers. This shallow understanding lacks the depth of a relationship

May we cling to the power of the cross in our times of trial.

WEEK THREE | DAY THREE

and is boiled down only to logic. But God is so much more than logic, as Job will soon help us see.

Bildad's final speech is the shortest of all the speeches and eloquently wraps up the arguments of Job's "comforters." For the first time, Bildad does not lecture Job about the peril of the wicked. Instead, he describes eternity. He describes the vastness of God: "Dominion and dread belong to him, the one who establishes harmony in his heights. Can his troops be numbered? Does his light not shine on everyone?" (Job 25:2–3). Yet Bildad's observation comes to an incorrect conclusion. Bildad asserts that because God is so vast, the everyday concerns of a man are too insignificant for God to worry about. Bildad describes the magnitude of God but misses His compassion.

Now that we understand Eliphaz's and Bildad's final speeches, let us observe Job's responses (found in chapters 23, 24, and 26). In Job's reply to Eliphaz, he recognizes two comforts: pleading his case before God and the judgment of the wicked. Job begins his response to Eliphaz by calling himself "bitter" (Job 23:2). This word "bitter" used here is the same word for "rebellious" in Hebrew, setting the tone for Job's risky desire to appear before God. Somehow, in the months of mourning and meditation, Job is convinced that his restoration is only found in the presence of God. Job believes that in the courtroom of God, he will be tested and "emerge as pure gold" (Job 23:10). However, not all of the world will receive that fate, for in Job 24, Job finds relief that one day God will judge those who oppress the weak and lowly. Ironically, these are the same sins that Eliphaz accuses him of committing. Like Eliphaz, Job agrees that these sins will one day meet the wrath of God. Perhaps Job is longing for a day when sin is obliterated from the earth. No longer will the wicked prosper or the evil sneak in the shadows; all will be exposed in the light of Christ.

Finally, Job responds to Bildad, ending the back-and-forth conversations between Job and his three friends. In Job's final response, he paints a picture of the majesty of God. But in this

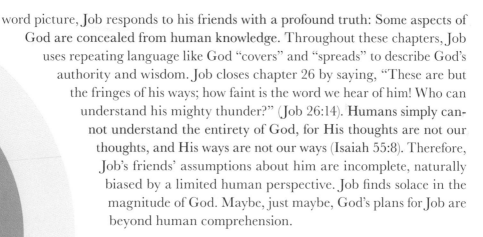

word picture, Job responds to his friends with a profound truth: Some aspects of God are concealed from human knowledge. Throughout these chapters, Job uses repeating language like God "covers" and "spreads" to describe God's authority and wisdom. Job closes chapter 26 by saying, "These are but the fringes of his ways; how faint is the word we hear of him! Who can understand his mighty thunder?" (Job 26:14). Humans simply cannot understand the entirety of God, for His thoughts are not our thoughts, and His ways are not our ways (Isaiah 55:8). Therefore, Job's friends' assumptions about him are incomplete, naturally biased by a limited human perspective. Job finds solace in the magnitude of God. Maybe, just maybe, God's plans for Job are beyond human comprehension.

Throughout the Old Testament, God's people received "faint whispers" of redemption—promises from God that one day hope would come. Hundreds of years later, these faint whispers turned into a shout of victory when an angel of the Lord declared, "He has risen!" on the glorious day of the resurrection (Matthew 28:6–7, Luke 24:6). The thunder of God's power is difficult to understand. In God's sovereignty, He sacrificed His only Son and then raised Him from the dead three days later. God's ways, much higher than our own, led Him to rescue His creation from their demise.

And so, Job completes his conversations with his exasperated friends. In many respects, Job is in the same place he started. He still sits in the ashes of a wasteland. He still has no answers from God. Yet, somehow, Job has emerged from his discourse more confident in his innocence and more desperate for God. Despite his questions and his accusations, Job displays for us the perseverance of a saint through trial. He has not abandoned God. He has not fallen deep into rebellion. He has kept his eyes glued to his only hope of future redemption—God. Like Job, may we cling to the power of the cross in our times of trial. Let our grip remain so firm, so steadfast, that our fingers abound with splinters and our knuckles go white. All other supports will fail, but the cross—the punishment of sin turned proclamation of salvation—will never give way.

1. Take a moment to reflect on the speeches of Eliphaz, Bildad, and Zophar. How would you describe the main points of their arguments?

2. How is Job "rebellious" in Eliphaz's eyes? How might placing your hope in the gospel be "rebellious" to our modern culture?

3. Reflect on Job's discourses throughout the book so far. How has Job grown in his understanding of his grief? How has he remained the same?

ATTRIBUTE OF GOD I'M MEDITATING ON TODAY

REMEMBER THIS

Job's Last Stand

In previous study days, we imagined the story of Job as a courtroom trial. Eliphaz, Bildad, and Zophar brought their best arguments against Job, belittling his suffering and demeaning his relationship with God. Job served as his own defense attorney, for he had no other human in his corner. God sat as the revered yet seemingly silent judge from whom Job longed to hear. In today's chapters, Job figuratively stands before this judge for his final deposition — his last-ditch effort to defend his innocence.

In fact, Job's innocence is his last prized possession on earth. He holds it as one would hold a precious jewel. In chapter 27, he says, "I will maintain my integrity until I die. I will cling to my righteousness and never let it go. My conscience will not accuse me as long as I live!" (Job 27:5b–6). The godless person has no chance of vindication, but Job believes there's hope for him. And so, with vigor and determination, Job makes his final appeal.

Before Job begins, we observe what reads like an intermission. Chapter 28 is a peaceful break from the growing tension between Job and his friends. Scholars fall into two separate camps when considering Job 28. Some believe that the author who penned Job inserted this poem to prompt reflection upon the end of discourses between Job and his friends. Others believe that Job 28 is a continuation of Job's speech in the previous chapter, as he expounds upon the majesty of God. No matter the opinion, we do know that all Scripture is inspired by God (2 Timothy 3:16). God included this chapter with intentionality and purpose — to help us meditate on the riches of His wisdom. The author equates the search for wisdom to mining for precious jewels. But no matter how hard we search, only "God understands the way to wisdom, and he knows its location" (Job 28:23). Job 28 reminds us that no man's wisdom is equivalent to God's — no matter how eloquent the argument or logical the explanation.

At the beginning of chapter 29, Job reminisces on the "good old days," before his life became overcome with tragedy. The order in which Job reflects reveals a great deal about his heart. His primary longing is a mended friendship with God (Job 29:2–6).

Jesus is God's comfort personified.

WEEK THREE | DAY FOUR

God watched over Job, shone His light upon Job's head, and dwelled with Job in fellowship. Job's heart was at rest. This description is a stark contrast to Job's current reality. Now God seems distant, and Job's heart is unsettled. One would expect the rest of Job's nostalgia to reflect on his family and wealth. But that does not seem to be what Job misses most. Job misses his influence—his ability to uplift and serve his community. Job's life, as described in this chapter, seems reminiscent of Jesus's two greatest commands: "Love the Lord your God with all your heart, with all your soul, and with all your mind" and "Love your neighbor as yourself" (Matthew 22:37, 39). Job's heart was aligned with the heart of God.

"But now . . ." The first two words of chapter 30 set the tone for the rest of Job's final plea. His new reality is a stark contrast to his "days of old" described in the previous chapter. Job describes his losses in three layers: external (verses 1–15), physical (verses 16–19), and spiritual (verses 20–31). His external loss is a loss of his reputation. Once, his community revered him; now, Job suffers ridicule. Even those "banished from human society" (verse 5) want nothing to do with him. Job describes himself as a city under attack by the very people who formerly begged for his wisdom. Next, he describes his physical turmoil. Let us not forget that Job still sits upon the ashes in unrelenting pain. Yet physical pain is not the worst of Job's problems; he also faces spiritual pain. The very God who was once his closest friend now will not answer his call. The darkness Job describes reminds us of his lament in chapter 3. Job still feels alone.

In chapter 31, Job asserts his innocence one last time. Job clears his name of any crime. It is as if Job reads a rap sheet of potential sins and clears himself of each one: lust, oppression, idolatry, selfishness, and hoarding of resources. Job's record is clean, and he hopes that his obedience is enough to warrant a reply from His Father. Through the course of Job's mourning, Job's assertion of innocence has made him more determined for answers and increasingly convinced that God will provide vindication. But as we will see, God will soon humble Job for his growing pride.

What are we to make of Job's last appeal to God? Job asks God to free him from his misery on the foundation of faith. Job has attentively lived a life of obedience. Yet through the course of his mourning, he has lifted his desire for innocence to match his desire for God. But above all, Job longs for comfort, a longing that is ultimately fulfilled in Christ. Jesus is God's comfort personified. He healed diseased bodies, cast out raging demons, and through his death, secured eternal comfort by cleansing Christians from sin. Even more, by His sacrifice, believers receive the Holy Spirit. Now, for those of us in Christ, God's comfort dwells within us always, teaching and reminding us of the hope we have in Christ (John 14:26). The comfort Job longed for—to rest again in the friendship of God—is offered to us by grace through faith in Jesus Christ.

In our seasons of grief, our feelings tell us that God is against us. Our feelings tell us that we are forgotten and unloved. Our feelings tell us that God is unfair. But if God is not fair, why would we trust Him? In the remainder of this book, Job will learn that God is not his enemy. God will bring forth eternal comfort through Job's temporary pain. As we begin the final stretch of Job, we will hone in on God's justice. We will see that God is not only just; He is intentional in the details, magnificent in power, and tender in forgiveness.

> FOR THOSE OF US IN CHRIST, GOD'S COMFORT DWELLS WITHIN US ALWAYS.

1. This is the last time Job will speak before he hears from God. Take a moment to summarize Job's defense or his argument for innocence. Do you believe he is right to approach God? Why or why not?

2. In chapter 29, Job reminisces about his life prior to his suffering. Read Isaiah 43:18–19. How might reminiscing on your past be dangerous? How might this distract you from the present or deter you from Christ?

3. Have your feelings ever seemed loud, even loud enough to drown out God? What do you do in these circumstances? How can you be grounded in truth in the future?

ATTRIBUTE OF GOD I'M MEDITATING ON TODAY

REMEMBER THIS

God's Forerunner: Elihu

PRACTICE THIS WEEK'S MEMORY VERSE + READ JOB 32–37

The figurative courtroom has come to silence. Both Job and his "comforters" have made their final remarks, and they are simply waiting on the judge to weigh in. But the silence is broken by a surprise witness. This witness is not a part of the prosecution or defense. Instead, Elihu weighs in from the audience, an onlooker who has silently observed the trial from beginning to end. From this point forward in the book of Job, the script flips. Thus far, Job has been our protagonist—the one we cheer for. But now, we will look upon God's chosen servant with loving criticism. Throughout Elihu's speeches, he attempts to help Job understand God's justice and glory.

Who is this man? And why does he speak up? Elihu is the youngest of the friends. This is why he waited until the end of their discourses to speak. In the first five verses of chapter 32, Elihu is described as "angry" four times. His anger burned against both Job and Job's friends. Job's friends could not silence Job and appropriately defend God's honor. And Elihu believes Job is worshiping his vindication above God. Thus, some scholars believe that Elihu's critique of Job serves an important role in setting the stage for God's coming speeches—some even call him a prophet. Yet we will see that, like Job's "comforters," Elihu makes false assumptions about Job, too. Though flawed, Elihu's speeches point us to a God who uses suffering to teach us more about Himself—a God whose ways are too magnificent to be questioned.

Elihu begins his speeches by first making a space for himself. Because of his youth, he is apprehensive to share (Job 32:6–7), but the "breath of the Almighty" propels him forward (Job 33:4). The theology he has heard thus far has angered him, and he cannot help but straighten what is crooked. Elihu promises to remain impartial. His motivation is simply to defend the character of God, and he does so in four speeches.

Elihu's First Speech (Chapter 33)

Unlike Eliphaz, Bildad, and Zophar, Elihu expresses compassion for the suffering cynic and first addresses Job. Elihu reminds him that God can communicate through suffering and perseverance. Elihu's argument sounds much like the Apostle Peter's in 1 Peter,

Jesus is the true and better mediator.

WEEK THREE | DAY FIVE

as he encourages the churches in Asia Minor to persevere through trial by writing, "though now for a short time, if necessary, you suffer grief in various trials so that the proven character of your faith—more valuable than gold, which, though perishable, is refined by fire—may result in praise, glory, and honor at the revelation of Jesus Christ" (1 Peter 1:6–7). Essentially, Elihu encourages Job to ask himself, *What might God be teaching me through this trial?*

Elihu's Second Speech (Chapter 34)

Elihu's second speech is addressed to Job's "comforters." He understands their frustration with Job. In Elihu's mind, Job has discounted the value of a relationship with God (Job 34:9). Job has accused God of not listening, of not being fair, and of enjoying the suffering of His children. Elihu does not believe these words can go unchallenged, for "it is impossible for God to do wrong, and for the Almighty to act unjustly" (Job 34:10). How can a sinful human challenge God's authority? Job's main flaw, according to Elihu, is that he has rebelled against God (Job 34:37). Yet Elihu is only partially correct. Yes, Job has accused God incorrectly, but in his heart, he has not rebelled against God in the way Elihu has suggested. Job has remained fixed and sure that God—not the world—holds the answers he longs for.

Elihu's Third Speech (Chapter 35)

Elihu again turns to Job to answer his question, *Why is God being silent?* Elihu believes that God will not answer someone who desires answers for his own gain. God honors the cries of those who come before him humbly and repentantly. Job, Elihu believes, comes before God in pride and arrogance, valuing his innocence over God Himself.

Elihu's Fourth Speech (Chapters 36-37)

In this speech, Elihu paints a picture of God's magnificence, and in doing so, he critiques Job's attempt to question God. Elihu describes God as mighty, understanding, just, sovereign, forgiving, and omnipotent (all-powerful). One can imagine that with this thoughtful description of God, Job's defenses slowly lower. "Can anyone understand how the clouds spread out or how the thunder roars from God's pavilion?" (Job 36:29). Amid Job's wrestling, Elihu stops and invites Job to "consider God's wonders" (Job 37:14). Elihu invites Job to step outside of his misery and worship.

Unlike the speeches of Eliphaz, Bildad, and Zophar, Job does not answer Elihu. Perhaps Elihu completed the task he set out to do—to humble Job before God's throne. Many scholars view Elihu as a sort of mediator, a man who paves the way for Job's meeting with God. Elihu may be a mediator, but he is not *the* Mediator. Elihu's insight is limited. He infers Job's heart, but he does not *know* Job's heart. He did not see Job's daily acts of faithfulness. He does not know that God Himself affirmed Job's innocence.

Jesus is the true and better mediator. Yes, Elihu may speak on behalf of God, but he cannot go to God on Job's behalf. Jesus can. Though Jesus cleansed us of our sins through His death and resurrection, He also continues to plead before the Father on behalf of sinners each day (Romans 8:34). Jesus is the embodiment of God's mercy, love, compassion, and faithfulness. Though Christ had not yet been revealed to mankind during Job's lifetime, God will soon show Job the love, compassion, and faithfulness that we now see in Jesus—God's own Son who took on the form of man (Philippians 2:6–7).

Elihu's speech reminds modern-day sufferers to remove our suffering from the throne of our hearts. Throughout Job's speeches, his desire to be declared innocent rose to match his love for God. Elihu reminds us of an important truth highlighted throughout Scripture: we shall worship no other gods but the one true God (Exodus 20:3–6).

Today, little "g" gods are not necessarily carved idols as described in the Old Testament. Examples of gods we may be tempted to worship can include our comfort, our relationships, our earthly securities, or our status. Are you coming to God to get the pain to stop or for more of Him? Are you truly trusting in His sovereign control, or are you holding on to control yourself? May we search our hearts and evaluate our motives for drawing near to God. Do we want what He gives us, or do we want Him? Let us heed the warning Elihu gives to Job. Because even if our pain never ends, even if the waiting is grueling, we have enough in Jesus.

1. Evaluate Elihu's criticisms of Job. What are they, and do you believe that they are fair?

2. Read the following verses: Proverbs 15:33, Matthew 23:12, and 1 Peter 5:5–6. What do these verses teach about humility? In seasons of suffering, why may it be more difficult to humble yourself?

ATTRIBUTE OF GOD I'M MEDITATING ON TODAY

REMEMBER THIS

*Think back on all of the Scripture that you read and studied
this week as you answer the questions below.*

What did you observe about God and His character?

What did you learn about the condition of mankind and yourself?

How does this week's Scripture point to the gospel?

How do the truths you have learned this week about God, man,
and the gospel give you hope, peace, or encouragement?

How should you respond to what you read and learned this week?
Write down one or two specific action steps you can take this week to apply what you learned.
Then, write a prayer in response to your study of God's Word.

Before we begin a new week of study, take some time to apply and share the truths of Scripture you learned this week. Here are a few ideas of how you could do this:

1. Schedule a meet-up with a friend to share what you are learning from God's Word.

2. Use these prompts to journal or pray through what God is revealing to you through your study of His Word.

   a. *Lord, I feel...*

   _____

   _____

   _____

   _____

   b. *Lord, You are...*

   _____

   _____

   _____

   _____

   c. *Lord, forgive me for...*

   _____

   _____

   _____

   _____

d. Lord, help me with…

_____

_____

_____

_____

3. Spend time worshiping God in a way that is meaningful to you, whether that is taking a walk in nature, painting, drawing, singing, etc.

4. Paraphrase the Scripture you read this week.

_____

_____

_____

_____

_____

_____

_____

5. Use a study Bible or commentary to help you answer questions that came up as you read this week's Scripture.

6. Take steps to fulfill the action steps you listed on Day 5.

7. Use highlighters to mark the places you see the metanarrative of Scripture in one or more of the passages that you read this week.
   (See the Metanarrative of Scripture on page 14.)

Scripture Memory

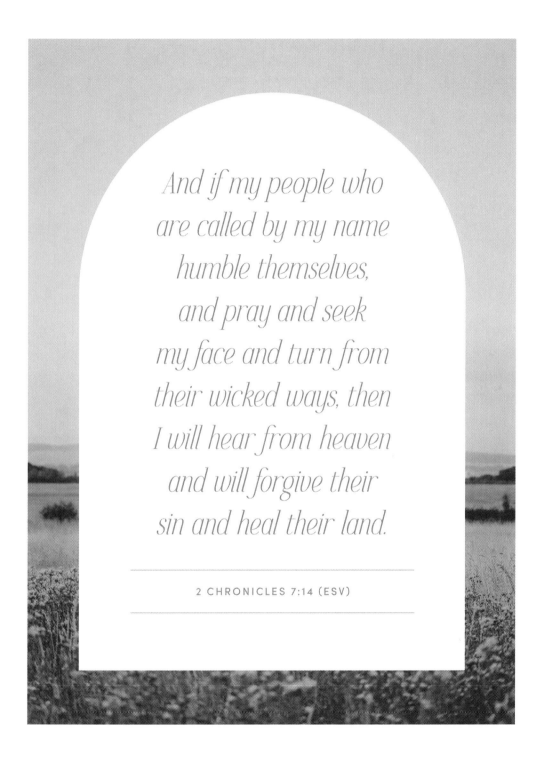

And if my people who are called by my name humble themselves, and pray and seek my face and turn from their wicked ways, then I will hear from heaven and will forgive their sin and heal their land.

2 CHRONICLES 7:14 (ESV)

God Meets With Job

Today is the moment Job has waited for. The day that prayers are answered. The day that strivings cease. God finally answers Job. Before we dive in, we must remember Job's current state. Job's heart is restless, tumbling in and out of anger and love for God, for he has both insulted God and praised His name. Festering sores cover Job from head to toe. His former friends are now his enemies. In the aftermath of his tragedies, Job feels alone and misunderstood. His former city taunts him in the distance, bustling unchanged. But for Job, everything has changed. The God he has spent his life serving now seems distant from his suffering. In desperation, he hurls complaints against God that likely feel familiar: *God, you have forgotten me! God, you are absent from my life! God, this pain I am feeling is your fault!* Job has called to God, but God has not answered. Until now.

God breaks the silence. The first verse of chapter 38 reads, "Then the LORD answered Job from the whirlwind" (Job 38:1). Does the wind sound familiar? The wind was the very tool Satan used to murder Job's children (Job 1:18–19). Now, God uses the wind to bring about Job's redemption. Before God even speaks a word, Job's healing begins. The very force that broke Job's heart is the force through which God mends it.

Throughout Job's suffering, he has asked God, "Why?" in various forms and in various ways. One would expect God to answer Job's questions or at least give him heavenly insight into his circumstances. Maybe God would explain that Job's testing was meant to encourage millions of people to persevere faithfully through their trials. Maybe God would share that it was not Him who afflicted Job but Satan. Maybe, just maybe, God would pronounce Job innocent, just as Job desires. But those answers are not what burst forth from the wind. The voice of God instead asks Job a long list of rhetorical questions. These questions showcase God's glory and might in the most majestic phenomena and the most minute details. In these questions, Job receives all the answers he needs.

God begins by answering a question you have likely wondered: *Is Job wrong for doubting God?* God answers this question by saying, "Who is this who obscures my counsel with

God worked all the pain in Christ's story to bring forth peace.

WEEK FOUR | DAY ONE

ignorant words?" (Job 38:2). He seems to be explaining, *You have no idea the depths of my knowledge or the breadth of my care!* The Apostle Paul expresses a similar understanding of God in his letter to the Roman church when he writes, "Oh, the depth of the riches and the wisdom and the knowledge of God! How unsearchable his judgments and untraceable his ways!" (Romans 11:33). Certainly, God's wisdom and knowledge is far above our own, so much that we cannot understand His judgments or His ways. So, as a loving father corrects a son, God does not simply tell Job he is wrong; He shows him a new way.

In chapter 38, God tours Job through the majestic wonders of His mighty creation. God showcases the mighty structures and systems of the universe. For example, God asks, "Where were you when I established the earth? Tell me, if you have understanding. Who fixed its dimensions? Certainly you know! Who stretched a measuring line across it?" (Job 38:4–5). God demonstrates that He alone sustains the earth. He alone determines the borders of the sea and the constellations of the sky. God zooms out, away from Job's tragedies, and shows Him the order He has created from chaos.

In chapter 39, God observes the details of creation—again by asking Job questions. For example, God asks, "Does the hawk take flight by your understanding and spread its wings to the south? Does the eagle soar at your command and make its nest on high?" (Job 39:26–27). God is sovereign over the mountain goats giving birth to new life, the wings of an ostrich flapping joyfully, and the horses romping in excitement. God's eye is on the sparrow, the oxen, the lion, and the lamb. In this chapter, God shows Job that He is not only in charge of the complex systems that govern the earth, but He is present in the most subtle details on earth. Surely, if God is keenly aware of the coming and going of these animals, He is alongside Job in every moment.

God's response is a reminder of His omnipresence—that He is everywhere at all times. He is with the patient who receives the crippling diagnosis. He is with the parent whose child tragically passes away. He is with the businessman who suddenly loses his

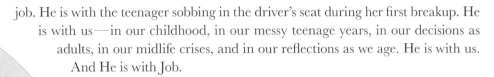

job. He is with the teenager sobbing in the driver's seat during her first breakup. He is with us—in our childhood, in our messy teenage years, in our decisions as adults, in our midlife crises, and in our reflections as we age. He is with us. And He is with Job.

God's questions are rhetorical, which means they do not require an answer. The answers are obvious. Job cannot control the rain or the thunder. He does not hold the secrets of the animal kingdom. Job is inferior to God. So are we. And that is a good thing.

God's answers to Job remind us that His thoughts are higher than our thoughts and His ways are higher than our ways (Isaiah 55:9)—a truth that we see expressed in the beauty of the gospel. For in God's infinite wisdom and knowledge, God chose to sacrifice His only Son for the forgiveness of sin. God chose for His Son to love though He was unloved and to be faithful among those who were faithless. He chose for His Son to suffer brutally on our behalf. Yet Scripture tells us, "For the joy that lay before him, he endured the cross, despising the shame, and sat down at the right hand of the throne of God" (Hebrews 12:2b). God worked all the pain in Christ's story to bring forth peace. So too, our suffering is never in vain. It is never meaningless. It is never unused or by mistake. God works all details together for our good and His glory (Romans 8:28). Let us be in awe of His sovereignty. As the famous hymn "His Eye Is on the Sparrow" reads:

"Let not your heart be troubled," His tender word I hear,
And resting on His goodness, I lose my doubts and fears;
Though by the path He leadeth, but one step I may see;
His eye is on the sparrow, and I know He watches me.

With profound lyricism, "His Eyes Is on the Sparrow" teaches us that we can find rest in God's never-changing character no matter our circumstances. God is good. He leads us. And because God's eye watches even the smallest creatures of creation, we can trust that He cares even more for us, who were made in His image (Matthew 10:29–31).

1. What does this passage teach you about God? How does resting in awe of God help us trust Him?

2. Why do you think God did not answer Job's questions directly? How does this provide Job with the real answers He needs?

3. Pick a verse or passage that puts you in awe of God. Take time this week to meditate on this verse and reflect on the majesty of God. Maybe this looks like watching a sunrise, meditating on your passage, or having a time of worship. Make your plan in the space below.

ATTRIBUTE OF GOD I'M MEDITATING ON TODAY

REMEMBER THIS

His Eye Is on the Sparrow

LYRICS BY: CIVILLA D. MARTIN / COMPOSED BY: CHARLES H. GABRIEL / DATE: 1905

"His Eye Is on the Sparrow" is a classic hymn that reminds us of God's care and provision for us, even in the most challenging circumstances. In fact, this song was inspired by a couple by the name of Mr. and Mrs. Doolittle, who faithfully served the Lord in joy though their realities were riddled with physical setbacks.

Civilla D. Martin, the author of this hymn, and her husband, Walter Stillman Martin, befriended Mr. and Mrs. Doolittle, whose lives demonstrated a deep reverence for God, in the early 1900s. Mr. Doolittle was paralyzed from the waist down, and his wife was bedridden for over twenty years. Despite their circumstances, this couple was known for their joy and care for others. Inspired by their faith in action, Mr. Martin asked them one day for the key to their happiness, and Mrs. Doolittle replied, "His eye is on the sparrow, and I know He watches me." Stunned by this simple, profound response, Mrs. Martin wrote the lyrics for what we now know to be "His Eye Is on the Sparrow."

Undoubtedly, Mrs. Doolittle's simple encouragement came from Matthew 10:29–31, which reads, "Aren't two sparrows sold for a penny? Yet not one of them falls to the ground without your Father's consent. But even the hairs of your head have all been counted. So don't be afraid; you are worth more than many sparrows."

Both this hymn and Matthew 10:29–31 deepen our understanding of God's speeches in Job. Though He does not directly answer Job's question — *Why did you allow me to go through this suffering?* — He answers Job with what he needs more: His presence. God's presence is with the sparrow. God's presence is with Job. God's presence is with you, too.

Why should I feel dis-cour-aged?___ Why should the shad-ows come?___
"Let not your heart be trou-bled,"___ His ten-der words I hear;___
When-ev-er I am tempt-ed,___ When-ev-er clouds a-rise,___

Why should my heart be lone-ly___ And long for heav'n and home___ When
And rest-ing on His good-ness,___ I lose my doubt and fear.___ Though
When songs give place to sigh-ing,___ When hope with-in me dies,___ I

Je-sus is my por-tion?___ My con-stant Friend is He:___ His
by the path He lead-eth___ But one step I may see:___ His
draw the clos-er to Him;___ From care He sets me free:___

eye is on the spar-row,___ And I know He watch-es me.___ His

eye is on the spar-row,___ And I know He watch-es me.___ I

sing be-cause I'm hap-py,___ I sing be-cause I'm free;___ For His

eye is on the spar-row,___ And I know He watch-es me.

Job Responds in Humility

The man of many words is finally silenced. God does what Job's friends could not do. Only God can bring the most prideful, stubborn hearts to humility. God's glory is finally revealed to Job. Job has tried to grasp it in past chapters, but now he finally sees it. Like a man waking up from a coma, Job begins to see the light of God. And it is far more glorious than he could have imagined.

In Job's final response to his friends, he spoke of God, saying, "How faint is the word we hear of him! Who can understand his mighty thunder?" (Job 26:14). Here, Job marveled at God's incomprehensible power and grandeur. Yet this mighty God reveals His presence to Job personally. God shows Himself true. God shows Himself faithful. God shows that He does listen and that He was, in fact, closer than Job's own breath throughout each moment of his agony.

Job is brought to humility in the presence of God. In Job 40:4a, Job says, "I am so insignificant. How can I answer you?" Throughout Job's discussions with his friends, he has been quick to speak, quick to retaliate, and quick to defend himself. But for the first time, Job admits he has nothing to offer. Job puts his hand over his mouth. Job's humility in the midst of God's glory reminds us of Isaiah's humbled response before God in Isaiah 6. In a vision, Isaiah enters the throne room of God and witnesses God's splendor. God's robe fills the temple, and winged angelic beings sing His praises. At the sound of their praises, the walls shake. Like Job, Isaiah experiences God's presence. And in God's presence, Isaiah says, "Woe is me for I am ruined because I am a man of unclean lips and live among a people of unclean lips, and because my eyes have seen the King, the LORD of Armies" (Isaiah 6:5). God's glory stuns Isaiah.

*Jesus is the true
and better Job.*

WEEK FOUR | DAY TWO

Isaiah is convicted of the uncleanliness of his lips and the lips of those who surround him—and rightfully so. The book of James describes how the tongue "stains the whole body, sets the course of life on fire, and is itself set on fire by hell" (James 3:6b). James goes on to claim that the tongue cannot be tamed, for blessing and cursing come out of the same mouth (James 3:8–10). With this perspective, we can understand why Job covers his mouth in response to God's glory. All of a sudden, the tongue that has sought innocence is now put on trial—is now found guilty. There are no more words to be said. There are no more defensive words to utter (Job 40:5).

In Job's newfound humility, he begins to understand his place before God. As an unholy human, Job is wrong to make demands before a holy God. As Derek Kidner states in his book *The Wisdom of Proverbs, Job, and Ecclesiastes*, God's speech "cuts us down to size, treating us not like philosophers but like children—limited in mind and puny in body—whose first and fundamental grasp of truth must be to know the difference between our place and God's and to accept it" (74). As infants lack the experience and wisdom to make their own decisions, we, too, lack perspective. We are in desperate need of the One who does hold all wisdom, the One who is our security and our safe place—God. It is this humility that Job finally grasps in his response.

Yet Job's answer is not enough. He has admitted his own inferiority before God, but this is only half of the work left to be done. Job's understanding of God's justice and sovereignty still needs to be reckoned with. Job has quieted himself but has not yet repented. As referenced in Kidner's quote, Job now understands his place as a child before his Father, but he has not fully accepted it. And so, in the next chapter, God will teach Job the breadth and depth of His power. As a result, Job's posture will be not only humbled but submitted to God's will and authority.

As we read Job's story, we may see many characteristics that mirror Jesus's story. Both were innocent sufferers, and both were misunderstood by those around them. Yet Jesus is the true and better Job. In Job's sufferings, he slowly began to idolize vindication and neglect the one true God. Yet soon, God's responses to Job will topple the walls of pride built around his heart. But Jesus never needed to be humbled. His existence is perfect humility on display. Philippians 2:6–8 says that though Jesus existed in the form of God, He "did not consider equality with God as something to be exploited. Instead he emptied himself by assuming the form of a servant, taking on the likeness of humanity. And when he had come as a man, he humbled himself by becoming obedient to the point of death—even to death on a cross." Jesus is God incarnate, God in flesh. Christ Jesus deserves all the praise the world can muster up, yet He submitted Himself to mockings, beatings, and crucifixion. Jesus did what Job could not do. He navigated His suffering with perfect humility.

May we learn from Job's mistakes and imitate Christ's humility. In the coming chapters, God speaks to Job again and continues to reveal His power and His justice. Though Job's humility has begun, God is still chiseling away the pride caked upon Job's heart. God is still waking Job from his metaphorical coma and revealing His light. Job's days of darkness are over, not because his circumstances have changed but because God has met with him. God has come close.

If you feel like God is far away from you today, consider Job. God does not leave him in lack. No, God gives Job more and more grace. He will speak to him again. God pursues Job's heart until he finally understands. God carries Job through. God is faithful to us today, just as He was faithful to Job. Keep praying. Keep seeking. Keep knocking, for as Jesus reminds us in Matthew 7:7–8, "Ask, and it will be given to you. Seek, and you will find. Knock, and the door will be opened to you. For everyone who asks receives, and the one who seeks finds, and to the one who knocks, the door will be opened." Keep seeking, friend. God does not allow His faithful ones to see decay but will instead fill you with the joy of His presence (Psalm 16:10–11).

1. Read Job 40:3–5 again. What is missing in Job's response? Do you neglect repentance in your own life? If so, pray Psalm 139:23–24. What sin or struggle can you bring to God today?

2. Read Psalm 16. In this psalm, David recounts that God does not abandon His children but instead will guide them and allow them to experience abundant joy in His presence. How does this psalm encourage you with God's nearness?

3. Consider Job's humility as compared to Jesus's humility. How does Jesus model perfect humility? How might you better incorporate humility into your life?

ATTRIBUTE OF GOD I'M MEDITATING ON TODAY

REMEMBER THIS

A Just and Sovereign God

PRACTICE THIS WEEK'S MEMORY VERSE + READ JOB 40:6–41:34

We began this study with a question: When your worst fears are realized and your nightmares see the light of day, where is God? Job has faced what he thought were his greatest fears: losing the comfort of his home, the laughter of his children, the security of his wealth, and the pride of his reputation. As Job sought answers in his grief, his desire to understand "why" usurped his reverence for God. In this chapter, God returns Job to his proper place — in awe and holy fear of his Maker. To do so, God describes two greater nightmares — beasts of His creation that are untamable by mankind. Through the descriptions of these beasts, God displays His power and control over evil.

God begins His speech in a similar manner to how He began the first: with a challenge. Throughout Job's longing for redemption, he was so determined to prove his innocence that he demeaned the authority of God. And God will not stand for it. Ironically, God offers to give Job exactly what he wants: the ability to administer justice. God says, "Would you declare me guilty to justify yourself? Do you have an arm like God's? Can you thunder with a voice like his? Adorn yourself with majesty and splendor, and clothe yourself with honor and glory. Pour out your raging anger; look on every proud person and humiliate him" (Job 40:8b–11). It is as if God offers to hand over His robe and His gavel.

In theory, administering justice is Job's ideal scenario. But no human can rule like God. We are weighed down by prejudices, selfish motives, and limited understanding. Though a toddler may try to walk in the boots of his father, he cannot lift the weight of such shoes with his infantile legs. The shoes are too big to fill. In the same way, Job cannot carry the weight of administering justice to the world. Throughout his

God holds supreme control over any threat in this world.

WEEK FOUR | DAY THREE

speeches, he has longed for the gavel, but God shows Job that the gavel rests in His only capable hands.

God continues His speech with detailed descriptions of two fearsome beasts: the Behemoth and the Leviathan. These beasts are special amongst creation because they are subdued by no one but God. These beasts are so frightening that scholars today still debate how exactly to understand them. Let us look at pages 160–161 before we speculate.

So what are Behemoth and Leviathan? Most scholars fall into either of two camps: that these creatures are real, created beings or that they are mythical creatures representing evil on the earth. Among scholars who believe Behemoth and Leviathan are real creatures, many believe that Behemoth is a hippopotamus and Leviathan is a crocodile. From this perspective, we must remember that social media, the Internet, and wildlife documentaries were not a part of ancient history. Job did not have experience with many of the vast array of creatures in God's creation. Therefore, staring into the faces of the hippopotamus and crocodile would likely evoke the kind of terror that brings Job to repentance.

Other scholars believe that Behemoth and Leviathan represent evil that roams the earth — specifically, death and Satan. In reference to Behemoth, scholars believe the author is describing death as an untamable, insatiable beast. One can imagine the grim reaper, lurking amongst the lotus plants and willow leaves (Job 40:22), ready to strike.

In Job, Leviathan is described as a sea dragon, for "smoke billows from his nostrils as from a boiling pot or burning reeds. His breath sets coals ablaze, and flames pour out of his mouth" (Job 41:20–21). In Psalms, Leviathan is described as a multiheaded sea monster crushed by God (Psalm 74:13–14), and in Isaiah 27:1, Leviathan is described as "the twisting serpent." Finally, this language finds completion in Revelation 12:9, when Scripture says, "So the great dragon was thrown out — the ancient serpent, who is called the devil and Satan,

the one who deceives the whole world. He was thrown to earth, and his angels with him" (Revelation 12:9, see also Revelation 20:2). From this point of view, God is communicating His power and authority over the most terrifying evils that plague the earth. Leviathan, or Satan, is subdued and subjected to God's authority. This complements the beginning of Job, for Satan could only attack Job with the permission of God (Job 1:12, 2:6).

Whatever your opinion on Behemoth and Leviathan, the take-away is the same; God holds supreme control over any threat in this world. God is sovereign; He knows all and can tame even the fiercest evils. And because God is sovereign, He is the only one capable of administering justice. Consider for a moment what would happen if Job did take the gavel and try out God's throne for a day; he might have erased his horrid experience from memory or maybe judged his friends for their lack of compassion. His rulings would likely be based on his personal agenda. A human in control would never choose to enact the gospel — to sacrifice their one and only beloved son to pay the penalty for sin. Only God, in His infinite wisdom and justice, would choose such a story. Our sin is costly, but God paid the price. Through Jesus, we are rescued from slavery and delivered into freedom.

Through God's final speech in the book of Job, Job is moved not necessarily to understanding but to trust. God is in control. Romans 8:38–39 communicates this truth as it says, "For I am persuaded that neither death nor life, nor angels nor rulers, nor things present nor things to come, nor powers, nor height nor depth, nor any other created thing will be able to separate us from the love of God that is in Christ Jesus our Lord." We have no need to fear; the beasts are tamed. In these chapters, God teaches Job that He has complete control and dominion over the most fear-provoking creatures and circumstances. God has control over Behemoth and Leviathan. He has control over Job's life. And He has control over yours.

1. Consider the differing opinions about Behemoth and Leviathan. Why can scholars disagree on details of Scripture yet Scripture still be true?

2. Throughout today's reading, God communicates that there are dangers in the world that are outside the control of man yet are like putty in His hands. Does this truth scare you or comfort you? What threats seem like Behemoth or Leviathan in your life right now? What does God say about these threats?

3. How can an understanding of God's sovereignty over evil allow you to rest, even in the most challenging circumstances?

ATTRIBUTE OF GOD I'M MEDITATING ON TODAY

REMEMBER THIS

BEHEMOTH

LEVIATHAN

Understanding Behemoth and Leviathan

Behemoth is a land animal that dwells by the river (Job 40:15, 23). It feeds on grasses and can almost never be satisfied with enough (Job 40:15). Behemoth ranks first among the beasts of God with incomparable strength (Job 40:19, 23). Even its belly, the most vulnerable spot of an animal, boasts powerful muscles (Job 40:16). Only its Maker, the God of the heavens and earth, can approach it with a sword (Job 40:19). Many scholars think that Behemoth is a hippopotamus.

Behemoth is not mentioned elsewhere in Scripture.

LEVIATHAN

Leviathan is a sea creature with a "layer of armor" (Job 41:13). Its mouth is like a set of doors, "surrounded by those terrifying teeth" (Job 41:14). Flames burst forth from its mouth and smoke from its nostrils (Job 41:19–20). This beast would make even the most legendary warriors terrified (Job 41:25). And even more importantly, if Job cannot capture or stand before Leviathan, how does Job (or anyone else!) expect to stand in the presence of God, Leviathan's maker? Leviathan is but clay in God's hands (Job 41:10). Many scholars believe that Leviathan may be a crocodile.

Other mentions of Leviathan in Scripture include Job 3:8, Psalm 74:14, Psalm 104:25–26, and Isaiah 27:1.

Understanding God's Justice

Mišpāṭ

JUDGMENT, JUSTICE

"Would you really challenge my justice?
Would you declare me guilty to justify yourself?"

JOB 40:8

In Job 40:8, God asks a question of Job that emphasizes a major theme throughout the book of Job: *is* God just? In fact, the Hebrew word for justice and judgment, *Mišpāṭ*, is repeated many times throughout Job. Throughout the study of Job, it is wise to develop an understanding of God's justice. In our limited perspectives, justice can be hard to understand. Often, human institutions of justice are riddled with corruption and ulterior motives.

However, God's justice contrasts the world's justice, for God's justice is infallible. Because God is holy and, therefore, sinless, His justice is perfect. He alone determines what is right and what is wrong (Deuteronomy 32:3–4). He executes judgment in fairness. He strengthens the faithful, uplifts the humble, and protects the persecuted. Conversely, He weakens the idolatrous, humbles the hardhearted, and punishes the persecutor.

Throughout Job, both Job and his friends wrestle with comprehending God's justice. In their understanding, God rewards the faithful and punishes the sinner. Job's friends argue that because Job has experienced tragedy, he must have committed an atrocious sin against God. Job, asserting that he is innocent while experiencing heartbreak, wrestles with a question that may be familiar, "Does God judge fairly?"

Throughout Job's tragedy and later redemption, God teaches Job that suffering can be used not as a punishment but as a way to strengthen the faith of a believer. Jesus, too, emphasizes this truth in John 16:33b, when He says, "You will have suffering in this world. Be courageous! I have conquered the world." Jesus's death and resurrection act in accordance with God's justice, for through this redemption, He welcomes the faithful into His eternal family. Jesus pays the debt for sin. He makes right what was wronged.

What about justice in our everyday lives? Often, we want judgment to be cast on what we cannot control—an evil leader in another country, a hurtful word said behind our back, or a perpetrator of a heinous crime. Desiring justice is a good, holy reflection of God's image inside us. And though it is noble and good to lift the oppressed and provide a voice for the voiceless, we must remember that ultimately, justice is not ours to administer (Romans 12:19). We cannot tame Behemoth or slay Leviathan. Only God can. And He will. Therefore, we are to trust in the hope given to Christians in the book of Revelation—Christ's second coming. Though we may not see God's ultimate judgment of evil in our lifetimes, we know it is coming. God promises heaven for His children and hell for those who refuse Him. He will welcome home the faithful into eternity while casting evil into utter darkness. God is fair. God is good.

> GOD'S JUSTICE CONTRASTS THE WORLD'S JUSTICE, FOR GOD'S JUSTICE IS INFALLIBLE.

Job's Repentance

Are you familiar with the Apostle Paul's conversion story? Before becoming the pro-lific church planter and evangelist we read about throughout the New Testament, Paul was once a feared enemy of Christians who did whatever he could to stop the spread of the gospel. He was a persecutor who breathed murderous threats against the disciples (Acts 9:1) and was complicit in the murder of at least one follower of Christ (Acts 7:58–8:1). However, God had redemption awaiting Paul, which we read about in Acts 9. In the midst of Paul's travels, he encountered Jesus in a blazing light. This light, the glory of Christ, blinded him. After three days of darkness, Scripture says that scales fell from Paul's eyes, and Paul's "sight" was never the same. Paul could not only physically see; he could spiritually see. Before, he had merely heard of Jesus, but upon this encounter, he saw Him as King of kings and Lord of lords. Similarly, God used Job's tragedies to open his spiritual eyes so that Job could better know Him.

Before we begin, let us recap God's speeches. It is important to remember that Job did not commit any sin to deserve his suffering. However, in his confidence of his innocence, God has chastised him for becoming prideful. Therefore, in the last few chapters, God, the Creator of heaven and earth, has spoken directly to Job.

To demonstrate His sovereignty, God has given Job a virtual tour of His creation, and along the way, Job has learned that God's wisdom and power are beyond his compre-hension. The weight of God's control is more than any human can fathom to lift. And therefore, the authority to give and to take, to build up and to destroy, to be silent and to speak remains only with God. He wields all things—good and evil—to bring about the redemption of the world. In today's verses, Job's response to finally understanding God's sovereignty leads him to worship, repentance, and a humbled posture before God.

Worship

Like scales fell from Paul's eyes after his conversion (Acts 9:18), metaphorical scales fall from Job's eyes in the aftermath of God's speech. Job cannot help but worship God, saying, "I know that you can do anything and no plan of yours can be thwarted"

We do not need answers. We do not need revenge or restitution. We need more of God.

WEEK FOUR | DAY FOUR

(Job 42:2). In Job's ignorance, he misunderstood God's silence for His absence. But God taught Job that He is keenly aware of every minute detail of His creation and in control of even the fiercest beasts. The only sensible response to the majesty and magnitude of God is praise. Scripture tells us that if Jesus's disciples were to stop praising God, the stones would worship Him instead (Luke 19:40). Creation was made to give God glory—so was Job, and so are we.

Repentance

What Job failed to do in his response to God's first speech (Job 40:3–5), he finally corrects in his second. Job repents. Repentance is the act of both confessing and turning away from sin in order to pursue obedience to God. In Job 42:3b, Job says, "Surely I spoke about things I did not understand, things too wondrous for me to know," and later, in verse 6a, he says, "Therefore, I reject my words and am sorry for them." Upon witnessing the glory of God, Job regrets his demanding stance before God. Who is he to demand a verdict? Who is he to claim innocence? Job recognizes that his pride usurped his worship of God. Often, we, too, can be guilty of demanding answers from God in the middle of our suffering. But true repentance lets go of the need for control. True repentance recognizes our blindness and trusts in the God who sees all, knows all, and upholds all.

Humbled Posture

Job closes his response to God by admitting, "I am dust and ashes" (Job 42:6). Remember, as Job witnesses God's glory veiled in the windstorm, he is still sitting among the dust and ashes outside of his city. Compared to God's glory, Job admits that he is no better than the dust and ashes that he sits upon. This is not a self-defeating posture but one that recognizes his proper place before God's throne. He is but a servant before a King. Job is no longer concerned with his vindication. The roar of his pride is silenced by the magnitude of God's glory. Maybe, after all this time, the sound of Job's pride was a

blind man's shout. Job did not need to be proven right; he needed to see God. This humility is a healthy posture for a believer. In Proverbs 22:4, humility is described as fear of the Lord. This fear is not the same as the fear one may have of heights or of snakes. This fear is reverence. Like Job, in order to humble ourselves, we must allow ourselves to be captivated by God's glory.

Let us remember that as Job utters this praise-filled apology to God, his circumstances have not changed. He still sits amidst the trash heap, covered in dust and ashes. He is still an outcast. He still does not have his answers. And yet, everything has changed—he once heard reports about God, but now he has seen God (Job 42:5). God is enough for Job. Job proves that he serves God for God Himself, not for personal gain or reward. Satan attempted to torture Job into cursing God. However, by experiencing God's glory, Job remains more confident in his faith than ever. Job proves that God's presence is enough for us in even the harshest of circumstances. We do not need answers. We do not need revenge or restitution. We need more of God.

Job's response shows us that, ultimately, the book of Job is not about Job or about suffering. The book of Job is about God. Job's friends asserted a simplistic view of God. Job asserted an incomplete view of God. But by the end of Job's story, Job (and readers) learn that God is much better at being in charge than we are. He is fair in justice. He is mighty in strength. He is perfectly sovereign—so much so that hundreds of years after Job's life, God revealed Himself again to humanity, but this time in the form of a man.

God's own Son, Jesus, was the image of the invisible God (Colossians 1:15). Through the life and works of Jesus, God's character is revealed to wayward, forgetful people. Like Job, in the glory of Christ, we should be brought to worship, repentance, and a humble posture, for through Christ, we commune with God and experience His glory daily through the presence of the Holy Spirit. Like Paul, the scales fall from our eyes. Like Job, we now see.

1. In your Bible, highlight evidence of Job's worship, repentance, and humbled posture in Job 42:1–6. (Maybe use three different colors!) Now read 2 Chronicles 7:14. What does God promise for those who repent? How does this encourage you?

2. Think about your current walk with the Lord. Is there anything you are struggling with? What would it look like for you to respond to Him in worship, repentance, and humility?

3. Take a moment to meditate on Job 42:5: "I had heard reports about you, but now my eyes have seen you." Have you had a moment in your faith journey when the gospel has become clearer to you? What was happening in your life during this season? What did you learn?

ATTRIBUTE OF GOD I'M MEDITATING ON TODAY

REMEMBER THIS

Job's Restoration

We love a good ending. At the end of a movie, we cheer when the underdog team wins the championship. At the end of a novel, we swoon when the prince carries his princess into a happily ever after. We love the tidiness of bow-tied conclusions. Job's story is no different, as many questions prompted by Job's trials are not answered until the epilogue, which we read today. *Is Job's relationship with God restored? Who was right about God—Job or his friends? Does Job's suffering end?* In Job 42:7–16, all of these questions find their answers. However, some of Job's implied questions will remain unanswered.

Why did God allow me to go through this?
Why does God allow His children to suffer?
Will anything good come out of these hard days?

It is here, in the tension of what God decides to answer and what He does not, that we find the buried treasure in the book of Job. Before we take a look at these unanswered questions, let us first take a look at how God concludes Job's story.

Is Job's Relationship with God Restored?

Four times within Job 42:7–8, God calls Job "my servant." This is a name reserved for honored patriarchs of our faith. Men like Abraham, Jacob, Moses, Caleb, David, and Isaiah, though imperfect, were examples to the Israelites—and to us—of genuine love for and trust in Yahweh. Job, too, is remembered as a servant of God. But we must remember that Job 42 is not the first time we see Job called God's "servant." In Job 1:8 and Job 2:3, when the Lord suggested Job for tempting by Satan, God said, "Have you considered my servant Job?" Therefore, upon the conclusion of Job, God faithfully accepts Job's repentance and once again calls Job his "servant."

God's response to Job's repentance reminds us that if we repent of our sins and turn toward God, He is faithful to forgive us, too. In 2 Chronicles 7:14, God speaks to Solomon concerning a wayward Israel and says, "If my people who are called by my name humble themselves, and pray and seek my face and turn from their wicked ways, then I

Job has shown us that God is all-powerful, all-knowing, and all-sufficient.

WEEK FOUR | DAY FIVE

will hear from heaven and will forgive them of their sin and heal their land" (ESV). God will not only forgive us, but He will heal our restless hearts with peace that surpasses understanding in a relationship with His Son, Jesus Christ. The weight you carry, the sadness you cannot seem to escape, and the anxiety that keeps you up at night can be laid to rest at the cross, for through Christ's death and resurrection, we are welcomed into the flock of a Good Shepherd. We are adopted as children of a loving Father.

Who Was Right About God – Job or His Friends?

In Job's conclusion, God offers forgiveness for Job's friends (Job 42:7–9). However, instead of asking them to repent of their own folly, God instructs them to offer sacrifices and ask Job to intercede (or pray to God) on their behalf. How humbling! God uses Job, the man they believed to be cursing God, to be a key that unlocks God's forgiveness for Job's friends. Referring to the trio, in Job 42:8, God says, "For you have not spoken the truth about me, as my servant Job has." Therefore, Job was correct about God, and his friends spoke falsely.

Like Jesus does throughout His ministry, God observes the hearts of these men. Throughout Job's sufferings, Job ceaselessly sought God's presence. He knew God alone held his answers. However, Eliphaz, Bildad, and Zophar relied on their own understandings and past precedents to inform their interpretation of God. They demeaned God's character by describing Him as one-dimensional and distant. And therefore, they misunderstood God's heart of compassion for the sufferer, patience for the sinner, and grace for those who repent.

Does Job's Suffering End?

Finally, as the book of Job closes, God restores Job's life to surpass its former splendor. God doubles Job's wealth, provides ten more children, and restores his prominence in the community. But it is important to remember two key truths about Job's returned prosperity. First, Job was fully satisfied with God's presence before his restoration. The camels and clout are nothing more than extra, for Job's prized possession is a restored relationship with God. And second, God does not bless Job out of a reward for his perseverance; God blesses Job out of His kindness and graciousness. Matthew 7:11 reminds us that God gives lavishly out of love for His children.

What About All the Unanswered Questions?

Though we have finished reading the book of Job, we must face the reality that Job never got all of his questions answered. We have no record of God ever informing Job about the heavenly conversation between Him and Satan (Job 1–2), nor do we ever see God provide Job with a reason for his suffering. However, God proved to Job that He is sovereign over all.

The truth is that humans have sought the knowledge of God ever since the garden of Eden. Satan tempted Adam and Eve with the knowledge of good and evil, and ever since their first bite of the forbidden fruit, mankind has wrestled with pushing against their God-given limits (Genesis 3). But what we fail to understand is that our limited knowledge was never a punishment but a gift. We are finite beings with finite minds who serve an infinite God of infinite knowledge. The truth buried in the book of Job is that our limited understanding of our suffering requires us to trust God with all our tomorrows. Through that trust, our relationship with Him is strengthened.

Job has shown us that God is all-powerful, all-knowing, and all-sufficient. Therefore, even in our unanswered questions, we can rest, for our God holds all victory over evil. He has cleansed our sin through the sacrifice of His Son, Jesus. And one day, in God's perfect timing, He will rid the world of evil once and for all (Revelation 20:10).

Just as God abundantly restored Job, Christ has secured for us a beautiful inheritance in heaven (Revelation 21:4). When we begin to believe there is no hope in sight, we can think about the gift of Jesus's presence, for Christ is with us when tears stream today, and He will be the One who wipes away our tears in eternity. The friend Job longed for throughout His suffering is the friend we have in Jesus Christ.

1. Reflect on the book of Job as a whole. What have you learned?
    How has your reverence for God deepened? How does the book
    of Job change your perspective of suffering?

2. Job finds contentment in God's presence before his family, his reputation,
    and his wealth are restored. What does this teach you about contentment
    in the Lord?

ATTRIBUTE OF GOD I'M MEDITATING ON TODAY

REMEMBER THIS

*Think back on all of the Scripture that you read and studied
this week as you answer the questions below.*

What did you observe about God and His character?

What did you learn about the condition of mankind and yourself?

How does this week's Scripture point to the gospel?

How do the truths you have learned this week about God, man,
and the gospel give you hope, peace, or encouragement?

How should you respond to what you read and learned this week?

Write down one or two specific action steps you can take this week to apply what you learned.
Then, write a prayer in response to your study of God's Word.

Job's Legacy

What would Job's gravestone read? Upon the conclusion of the book of Job, you may have a few ideas. In the final sentence of the book of Job, we gain an even better insight.

"THEN JOB DIED, OLD AND FULL OF DAYS."

JOB 42:17

Though this may seem like a simple sentence, it holds great meaning. It is Job's epitaph. An epitaph is a phrase or sentence written in memory of one who has died. This epitaph uses similar language to what Scripture uses to describe some of God's most faithful servants. (For example, Abraham in Genesis 25:8, Isaac in Genesis 35:29, David in 1 Chronicles 29:28, and the priest Jehoiada in 2 Chronicles 24:15.) Though Job's life does not exist in the redemptive storyline of Israel, his inclusion among the patriarchs points to God's greater redemptive purpose—to welcome people from every nation, tribe, and language into His covenantal family (Revelation 7:9). Even in the Old Testament, God's plan of redemption was a global one.

But Job's memorial does not stop there. In the New Testament, James honors Job in James 5:11: "See, we count as blessed those who have endured. You have heard of Job's endurance and have seen the outcome that the Lord brought about—the Lord is compassionate and merciful." Though Job experienced the depth of the valley, he is remembered as one who persevered by keeping his eyes fixed on God. Even when Job doubted, he knew that God was his only comfort. May we, like Job, entrust our suffering to the God who is able to bring beauty from ashes and multiply that beauty throughout generations. Job's legacy is one of endurance.

Job 42:17

Genesis 25:8   Genesis 35:29   1 Chron. 29:28   2 Chron. 24:15

Suffering and the Gospel

*What Does the Gospel Say About
Suffering in Our Lives Today?*

1. **WE DO NOT HAVE TO BE SURPRISED BY SUFFERING.** Before Jesus ascended into heaven to be with His Father, He prepared His disciples for future ministry: "You will have suffering in this world. Be courageous! I have conquered the world" (John 16:33b). Jesus confirms here that His good and faithful servants will limp through their time on earth. They will face trial—and not only trial but persecution because they are Christians. But Jesus did not leave them without hope. As Job learned, Jesus encouraged His disciples that He has conquered the world. He holds control over evil. And therefore, any suffering that comes into our lives is divinely allowed, controlled, and ultimately conquered by our Lord Jesus. We have no need to fear.

2. **THROUGH SUFFERING, WE COMMUNE WITH CHRIST.** Jesus did not promise suffering for His disciples without first modeling perseverance through suffering throughout His own life. In Isaiah 53:3 (ESV), Isaiah prophesied that Jesus would be a "man of sorrows and acquainted with grief." Jesus was betrayed, mocked, despised, beaten, pierced, and murdered in His lifetime here on earth. Jesus experienced the full gamut of emotional and physical pain. Yet, in all this suffering, He did not stray from His Father. In our times of suffering, we gain a deeper appreciation and reverence for our King and Comforter. Our suffering is communion with Christ, for we gain an opportunity to feel what He felt and to endure what He endured. We gain a taste of the price He paid to set us free from sin. Therefore, our worship is deepened, and our love for Him grows ever more strong. Through Jesus's personal experience of pain, we gain His eternal presence and entrance into His kingdom of peace and perfection. By His wounds, we are healed (Isaiah 53:5).

3. **THROUGH SUFFERING, OUR FAITH IS STRENGTHENED.** As a diamond is formed by the pressure of the earth, so, too, our faith is formed through the pressure of trial. Throughout our lives as Christians, the Holy Spirit sanctifies our hearts,

transforming us to look more and more like Jesus. This sanctification does not happen overnight but through patient endurance and faithfulness throughout our lives. Often, our faith hits a growth spurt in seasons of suffering. We come face to face with the truth: that we are weak, and God is strong. Like Job, we are humbled to repent of our pride and admit that we do not hold the answers within ourselves. We learn that God alone holds control. And in that newfound humility, God is elevated above the chaos of our circumstances. It is here, in the intersection of understanding God's sovereign control and knowing His compassionate character, where we find the confidence to persevere. God was faithful to redeem His children through Jesus Christ, and He will be faithful to deliver His children into peace with Him in eternity.

4. THROUGH SUFFERING, WE LEARN THAT CHRIST IS ENOUGH. Romans 5:3–5 reminds us that hope produced through faithful endurance will never disappoint us, for this hope is not hinged on changing circumstances but on the sure and steadfast promise that Christ has overcome the world. In our suffering, we are reminded that no relationship, no job, no amount of money, and no illusion of control is capable of fixing our broken hearts. No earthly reward can calm our restlessness or answer the question, "Why, God?" Only in the presence of God do we find the rest and the answers we desire. Only in the gospel do we find healing for our shame, strength for our weakness, and lasting hope for tomorrow. Perhaps words cannot describe the mystery of Christ's nearness to the suffering servant of God. But it is real, it is compassionate, and it is enough. Christ is closer to us than any friend or family member because He dwells within us through His Holy Spirit. It is in His nearness—it is in the presence of Christ—that our questions cease, for we are held secure in His hands. As we persevere, we can cling to the promise that what we taste of Christ now, we will savor in full in His presence for eternity (Revelation 21).

66

I waited patiently for the LORD, and he turned to me and heard my cry for help. He brought me up from a desolate pit, out of the muddy clay, and set my feet on a rock, making my steps secure. He put a new song in my mouth, a hymn of praise to our God. Many will see and fear, and they will trust in the LORD.

PSALM 40:1–3

As this study comes to an end, take some time to apply and share the truths of Scripture you learned this week and throughout the entire study. Here are a few ideas of how you could do this:

1. Schedule a meet-up with a friend to share what you are learning from God's Word.

2. Use these prompts to journal or pray through what God is revealing to you through your study of His Word.

    a. *Lord, I feel...*

    _____

    _____

    _____

    _____

    b. *Lord, You are...*

    _____

    _____

    _____

    _____

    c. *Lord, forgive me for...*

    _____

    _____

    _____

    _____

d. Lord, help me with…

_____

_____

_____

_____

3. Spend time worshiping God in a way that is meaningful to you, whether that is taking a walk in nature, painting, drawing, singing, etc.

4. Paraphrase the Scripture you read this week.

_____

_____

_____

_____

_____

_____

_____

5. Use a study Bible or commentary to help you answer questions that came up as you read this week's Scripture.

6. Take steps to fulfill the action steps you listed on Day 5.

7. Use highlighters to mark the places you see the metanarrative of Scripture in one or more of the passages that you read this week.
(See the Metanarrative of Scripture on page 14.)

What is *the* Gospel?

Thank you for reading and enjoying this study with us! We are abundantly grateful for the Word of God, the instruction we glean from it, and the ever-growing understanding it provides for us of God's character. We are also thankful that Scripture continually points to one thing in innumerable ways: the gospel.

We remember our brokenness when we read about the fall of Adam and Eve in the garden of Eden (Genesis 3), where sin entered into a perfect world and maimed it. We remember the necessity that something innocent must die to pay for our sin when we read about the atoning sacrifices in the Old Testament. We read that we have all sinned and fallen short of the glory of God (Romans 3:23) and that the penalty for our brokenness, the wages of our sin, is death (Romans 6:23). We all need grace and mercy, but most importantly, we all need a Savior.

We consider the goodness of God when we realize that He did not plan to leave us in this dire state. We see His promise to buy us back from the clutches of sin and death in Genesis 3:15. And we see that promise accomplished with Jesus Christ on the cross. Jesus Christ knew no sin yet became sin so that we might become righteous through His sacrifice (2 Corinthians 5:21). Jesus was tempted in every way that we are and lived sinlessly. He was reviled yet still yielded Himself for our sake, that we may have life abundant in Him. Jesus lived the perfect life that we could not live and died the death that we deserved.

The gospel is profound yet simple. There are many mysteries in it that we will never understand this side of heaven, but there is still overwhelming weight to its implications in this life. The gospel tells of our sinfulness and God's goodness and a gracious gift that compels a response. We are saved by grace through faith, which means that we rest with faith in the grace that Jesus Christ displayed on the cross (Ephesians 2:8–9). We cannot save ourselves from our brokenness or do any amount of good works to merit God's favor. Still, we can have faith that what Jesus accomplished in His death, burial, and resurrection was more than enough for our salvation and our eternal delight. When we accept God, we are commanded to die to ourselves and our sinful desires and live a life worthy of the calling we have received (Ephesians 4:1). The gospel compels us to be sanctified, and in so doing, we are conformed to the likeness of Christ Himself. This is hope. This is redemption. This is the gospel.

GENESIS 3:15

I will put hostility between you and the woman, and between your offspring and her offspring. He will strike your head, and you will strike his heel.

ROMANS 3:23

For all have sinned and fall short of the glory of God.

ROMANS 6:23

For the wages of sin is death, but the gift of God is eternal life in Christ Jesus our Lord.

2 CORINTHIANS 5:21

He made the one who did not know sin to be sin for us, so that in him we might become the righteousness of God.

EPHESIANS 2:8-9

For you are saved by grace through faith, and this is not from yourselves; it is God's gift — not from works, so that no one can boast.

EPHESIANS 4:1-3

Therefore I, the prisoner in the Lord, urge you to walk worthy of the calling you have received, with all humility and gentleness, with patience, bearing with one another in love, making every effort to keep the unity of the Spirit through the bond of peace.

BIBLIOGRAPHY

SOURCES USED THROUGHOUT THE STUDY

Allen, David L. *Christ-Centered Exposition: Exalting Jesus in Job*. Nashville: B&H Publishing Group, 2022.

Andersen, Francis I. *Job: An Introduction and a Commentary*. Vol. 14. Tyndale Old Testament Commentaries. Downers Grove, IL: Inter-Varsity Press, 1976.

Ash, Christopher. *Job: The Wisdom of the Cross*. Preaching the Word Series. Wheaton, IL: Crossway, 2014.

Dennis, Lane T., and Wayne Grudem, ed. *The ESV Study Bible*. Wheaton, IL: Crossway, 2008.

Hartley, John E. *The Book of Job*. Grand Rapids, MI: William B. Eerdmans Publishing Company, 1988.

SOURCES USED FOR WEEK 1

Collins, John, and Tim Mackie. "Overview: Job." *BibleProject*. October 22, 2015. YouTube video, 11:00. https://www.youtube.com/watch?v=xQwnH8th_fs/.

Mackie, Tim. "God's Response to Job's Questions About Suffering: God Knows Exactly What He's Doing" *BibleProject Blog*. Bible Project. 2017. https://bibleproject.com/blog/gods-gives-job-tour-wise-world/.

Vroegop, Mark. *Dark Clouds, Deep Mercy: Discovering the Grace of Lament*. Wheaton, IL.: Crossway, 2019.

SOURCES USED FOR WEEK 2

Baldwin, Susanna. "Miserable but Not Monochrome: The Distinctive Characteristics and Perspectives of Job's Three Comforters." *Themelios*. The Gospel Coalition. April 2018. https://www.thegospelcoalition.org/themelios/article/miserable-but-not-monochrome-the-distinctive-characteristics-and-perspectiv/.

SOURCES USED FOR WEEK 3

Only the sources mentioned in the "Sources Used Throughout the Study" section were used for Week 3.

SOURCES USED FOR WEEK 4

Fenner, Chris. "His Eye Is on the Sparrow." *Hymnology Archive*. April 20, 2020. https://www.hymnologyarchive.com/his-eye-is-on-the-sparrow.

Kidner, Derek. *The Wisdom of Proverbs, Job and Ecclesiastes*. Westmont, IL: IVP Academic, 1985.

Martin, Civilla D. "His Eye is on the Sparrow." *Hymnary*. 1905. Accessed March 27, 2023. https://hymnary.org/text/why_should_i_feel_discouraged#instances.

Merriam-Webster.com Dictionary, s.v. "Epitaph." Accessed October 28, 2022. https://www.merriam-webster.com/dictionary/epitaph.

Piper, John. "Job: The Revelation of God in Suffering." *Desiring God*. Desiring God. July 28, 1985. https://www.desiringgod.org/messages/job-the-revelation-of-god-in-suffering.

*Thank you for studying
God's Word with us!*

CONNECT WITH US
@thedailygraceco
@dailygracepodcast

CONTACT US
info@thedailygraceco.com

SHARE
#thedailygraceco

VISIT US ONLINE
www.thedailygraceco.com

MORE DAILY GRACE
Daily Grace® Podcast